Mortal Beauty,
God's Grace

VINTAGE SPIRITUAL CLASSICS

General Editors
John F. Thornton
Susan B. Varenne

ALSO AVAILABLE

The Bhagavad Gita
The Book of Job
Buddhist Wisdom: The Diamond Sutra and The Heart Sutra
The Confessions of Saint Augustine
The Desert Fathers
Devotions Upon Emergent Occasions
The Essential Gandhi
Faith and Freedom: An Invitation to the Writings of Martin Luther
The Imitation of Christ
Introduction to the Devout Life
John Henry Newman: Selected Sermons, Prayers, and Devotions
The Little Flowers of St. Francis of Assisi
Practical Mysticism and Abba
The Rule of St. Benedict
Saint Thomas More: Selected Writings
A Serious Call to a Devout and Holy Life
The Spiritual Exercises of St. Ignatius
Wells of Living Water: The Five Scrolls
The Wisdom of John Paul II

Mortal Beauty, God's Grace

Major Poems and Spiritual Writings

of Gerard Manley Hopkins

EDITED BY

John F. Thornton and *Susan B. Varenne*

PREFACE BY

Brad Leithauser

VINTAGE SPIRITUAL CLASSICS

VINTAGE BOOKS

A DIVISION OF RANDOM HOUSE, INC.

NEW YORK

S/O M-W 8/04 12.35

A VINTAGE SPIRITUAL CLASSICS ORIGINAL, DECEMBER 2003
FIRST EDITION

Library of Congress Cataloging-in-Publication Data
Hopkins, Gerard Manley, 1844–1889
Mortal beauty, God's grace : major poems and spiritual writings of Gerard Manley Hopkins /
edited by John F. Thornton and Susan B. Varenne ; preface by Brad Leithauser.—1st ed.
p.   cm.—(Vintage spiritual classics)
Includes bibliographical references (p.).
ISBN 0-375-72566-0
1. Christian poetry, English.   2. Spiritual life—Poetry.   3. Spiritual life.   I. Thornton,
John F., 1942–   II. Varenne, Susan B.   III. Title.   IV. Series.
PR4803.H44A6   2003
821'.8—dc21

2003057156

Book design by Fritz Metsch

www.vintagebooks.com

Printed in the United States of America
10   9   8   7   6   5   4   3   2   1

CONTENTS

by John F. Thornton and Susan B. Varenne, General Editors

A turn or shift of sorts is becoming evident in the reflections of men and women today on their life experiences. Not quite as adamantly secular and, perhaps, a little less insistent on material satisfactions, the reading public has recently developed a certain attraction to testimonies that human life is leavened by a Presence that blesses and sanctifies. Recovery, whether from addictions or personal traumas, illness, or even painful misalignments in human affairs, is evolving from the standard therapeutic goal of enhanced self-esteem. Many now seek a deeper healing that embraces the whole person, including the soul. Contemporary books provide accounts of the invisible assistance of angels. The laying on of hands in prayer has made an appearance at the hospital bedside. Guides for the spiritually perplexed have risen to the tops of best-seller lists. The darkest shadows of skepticism and unbelief, which have eclipsed the presence of the Divine in our materialistic age, are beginning to lighten and part.

If the power and presence of God are real and effective, what do they mean for human experience? What does He offer to men and women, and what does He ask in return? How do we recognize Him? Know Him? Respond to Him? God has a reputation for being both benevolent and wrathful. Which will He be for me and when? Can these aspects of the Divine somehow be reconciled?

Where is God when I suffer? Can I lose Him? Is God truthful, and are His promises to be trusted?

Are we really as precious to God as we are to ourselves and our loved ones? Do His providence and amazing grace guide our faltering steps toward Him, even in spite of ourselves? Will God abandon us if the sin is serious enough, or if we have episodes of resistance and forgetfulness? These are fundamental questions any person might address to God during a lifetime. They are pressing and difficult, often becoming wounds in the soul of the person who yearns for the power and courage of hope, especially in stressful times.

The Vintage Spiritual Classics present the testimony of writers across the centuries who have considered all these difficulties and who have pondered the mysterious ways, unfathomable mercies, and deep consolations afforded by God to those who call upon Him from out of the depths of their lives. These writers, then, are our companions, even our champions, in a common effort to discern the meaning of God in personal experience. For God is personal to us. To whom does He speak if not to us, provided we have the desire to hear Him deep within our hearts?

Each volume opens with a specially commissioned essay by a well-known contemporary writer that offers the reader an appreciation of its intrinsic value. A chronology of the general historical context of each author and his work is provided, as are suggestions for further reading.

We offer a final word about the act of reading these spiritual classics. From the very earliest accounts of monastic practice—dating back to the fourth century—it is evident that a form of reading called *lectio divina* ("divine" or "spiritual reading") was essential to any deliberate spiritual life. This kind of reading is quite different from that of scanning a text for useful facts and bits of information, or advancing along an exciting plotline to a climax in the action. It is, rather, a meditative approach by which the reader seeks to savor and taste the beauty and truth of every phrase and passage. This process of contemplative reading has the effect of enkindling in the reader compunction for past behavior that has been less than beautiful and true. At the same time, it increases the desire to seek a realm where all that is lovely and unspoiled may be found. There are four steps in *lectio divina:* first, to read, next to meditate, then to rest in the sense of God's nearness, and, ultimately, to resolve to govern one's actions in the light of new understanding. This kind of reading is itself an act of prayer. And, indeed, it is in prayer that God manifests His Presence to us.

PREFACE TO THE VINTAGE
SPIRITUAL CLASSICS EDITION

by Brad Leithauser

Of the English poet Gerard Manley Hopkins it might be said that he's difficult only if you try to understand him. A reader might reasonably choose not to. Certainly there are moments—as when you hit a phrase like "Or a jaunting vaunting vaulting assaulting trumpet telling"—whose passionate clamor makes any cool search for meaning look finicky and small-minded.

Perhaps it's a matter of taking the long view. Hopkins devoted his entire adult life to the Catholic Church, converting from his family's High Anglicanism at the age of twenty-two and eventually becoming a Jesuit priest. It's hardly unexpected that theories of art for art's sake held no appeal for him, given that all art, all everything, derives from God. Nor, under these circumstances, is the notorious obscurity of some of his poems all that surprising, since all mysteries are unriddled in God's eye.

Yet the more you read Hopkins, the clearer it grows how fervently he longed for understanding readers. Although his entire literary lifetime unfolded during Queen Victoria's reign (his earliest schoolboy verses were composed in the 1860s; his final poem, a sonnet addressed to his friend and literary executor, Robert Bridges, was composed just before his death, of typhus, in 1889), critics frequently group him with his knotty modernist successors like Ezra Pound and T. S. Eliot. They do so partly because of his experimental prosody, with its protracted lines and syncopated stresses, and partly because of his delayed publishing history. (The first collection of Hopkins's poetry, under Bridges's editorship, did not surface until 1918.) To view Hopkins as a twentieth-century poet often makes a good deal of sense (just as it makes sense to treat William Blake's actual birth date—1757—as a historical accident and to fold him into the nineteenth century). Surely a phrase of Hopkins's like "that side hurling a heavyheaded hundredfold / What while we, while we slumbered," from "The Leaden Echo and the Golden Echo," bears a closer resemblance to e. e. cummings than to anything else in the nineteenth century; the creatures in a line like "As kingfishers catch fire, dragonflies draw flame," from one of his most famous sonnets, feel more like denizens of one of Marianne Moore's bestiaries than William Wordsworth's. And yet Hopkins showed little tolerance for what would be, in the next century, the modernists' common acceptance of obscurity—especially the idea that certain emotional states are necessarily, rightly ineffable. (It's hard to picture Eliot or Pound or Moore doing what Hopkins regularly did when Bridges complained a passage was opaque—he would obligingly supply an abundant prose paraphrase—or to picture them meticulously anno-tating, as Hopkins did, with accents, double accents, and half a dozen other diacritical marks, how he wished a poem to be read aloud.) Even when Hopkins's words hurtle like a river in spate, he can be counted on to have in mind something quite specific that he longs to impart.

This sense of arcane but discoverable meanings lends an air of sharp decisiveness to minute matters of Hopkins criticism. The notes to the most recent Oxford University Press edition of the com-plete poems (1990) offer learned ornithological debate over what is going on, aerodynamically, with the kestrel glimpsed in the first stanza of "The Windhover":

I caught this morning morning's minion, king-
 dom of daylight's dauphin, dapple-dawn-drawn Falcon, in his
   riding
Of the rolling level underneath him steady air, and striding
High there, how he rung upon the rein of a wimpling wing
In his ecstasy!

What exactly does it mean for a bird to have "rung upon the rein of a wimpling wing"? Such discussions have point and meaning only if Hopkins's words are more than words—if, behind all his verbal arabesques, you behold a real bird doing real things.

Predictably, Hopkins's penchant for some irreducible, literal subject matter had religious underpinnings. He wasn't merely uninterested in but was censorious of any poetry divorced from the world, as his scattered grumblings about Algernon Charles Swinburne reveal. (In perhaps the last of these, he wrote to Bridges: "It is all now a 'self-drawing web'; a perpetual functioning of genius without truth, feeling, or any adequate matter to be at function on.") Swinburne was insufficiently earnest—a word that, despite its stuffy overtones for modern readers, denoted for Hopkins that combination of gravity, sincerity, and penetration from which most art springs. If our primary human duty is, as he once wrote, to "give God glory and to mean to give it," any strain of poetry that fares too far from the world of His creation risks flightiness, if not ingratitude.

Hopkins saw the very notion of "religious poetry" as something of a pleonasm—a favorite term of his when dismissing somebody's laxity of thought. While art for art's sake was predictably far from his interest, the degree to which Hopkins chose to make a spiritual virtue of sharp-sightedness was not necessarily to be expected. But in a private world like his, where a tiny and easily overlooked blue-bell could ring out a message of divine reassurance—he knew "the beauty of our Lord by it"—alert observation became not merely a gratification but a joyfully embraced responsibility.

In one of his sermons Hopkins spoke of the world as "word, expression, news from God." Surely, given their source, no such bulletins should ever be overlooked, and we are all bound to constant vigilance. (Or, as he tersely put it, chronicling the day's weather in one of his journals: "There were both solar and lunar halos, faint: it deserves notice.") He was pleased to discover "nothing at random" in even the most out-of-the-way places, as another journal entry makes clear:

> Looking down into the thick ice of our pond I found the imprisoned air-bubbles nothing at random but starting from centres and in particular one most beautifully regular white brush of them, each spur of it a curving string of beaded and diminishing bubbles.

This notion of an imposed watchfulness may help to explain Hopkins's passion for ephemera. He was a great one for studying, with a scientist's calibrating eye, phenomena like melting crystals, rainbows, lightning, rising steam clouds, the iridescence of a pigeon's neck. The vocabulary of his observations often bore a scientific tinge: "the laws of the oak leaves," "horizontally prolate gadroons," "very plump round clouds something like the eggs in an opened ant-hill." Indeed, in many of his journal entries he sounds far closer in spirit to his troubling Victorian contemporary Charles Darwin than to anything we'd expect from a poet-priest. Of all passing natural phenomena, drifting clouds drew him most profoundly, their never-to-be-duplicated patterns serving as one-time-only jottings on the chalkboard of the sky.

Hopkins modestly spoke of his "weather journal," though its range of entries extended far beyond the sky's doings. No series of excerpts could do justice to this collection of quiet observations, whose effect depends on an impression of dailiness, of steady aggregation. It certainly sounds surpassingly tedious—a diary of weather conditions compiled by a mostly unpublished priest-with-literary-leanings.

The journal offers little in the way of religious comment—there is little abstract musing of any sort. (It should be noted that Hopkins kept other, presumably more intimate journals that were deliberately destroyed, either by Hopkins or by those seeking to protect his memory; the portrait we're left with is fascinatingly fragmentary.) On most of his journal pages there is simply an eye, roving over a largely tame English rural landscape. Admittedly, it's sometimes difficult to tell precisely what phenomenon Hopkins is describing. Just as ornithologists may argue over the windhover's flight, meteorologists could have a field day sorting out some of his more eccentric annotations:

> Standing on the glacier saw the prismatic colours in the clouds, and worth saying what sort of clouds: it was fine shapeless skins of fretted make, full of eyebrows or like linings of curled leaves which one finds in shelved corners of a wood.

But if readers can't always picture the cloudscapes Hopkins so painstakingly sets before them, the journal delivers something rarer and more inspiring yet: all the minute observations eventually add up to a vision of the world, and a portrait of the retiring man himself, in all his potent susceptibilities and vulnerablities, his rapturous excitements and self-imposed asceticism. (It's no wonder that another keen-eyed inspector of minutiae, Elizabeth Bishop, was obsessed with these journals.) His first glimpse of the northern lights is particularly memorable:

> This busy working of nature wholly independent of the earth and seeming to go on in a strain of time not reckoned by our reckoning of days and years but simpler and as if correcting the

preoccupation of the world by being preoccupied with and appealing to and dated to the day of judgment was like a new witness to God and filled me with delightful fear.

If Hopkins witnessed God in the skies, a reader may behold in his journals one of the gods—one of the immortals of English poetry—likewise revealing himself through an implicit immanence.

2

Little in Hopkins's background, beyond his family's general interest in culture, would suggest the makings of a revolutionary writer. Born in 1844 at Stratford in Essex, he was the eldest of nine children. Hopkins's father, a specialist in marine insurance, occasionally composed highly conventional verses. Two brothers became commercial artists.

Hopkins's first significant act of rebellion was not artistic but religious: he was still a student at Oxford when he converted to Roman Catholicism—a life-transforming decision from which he never wavered. In the wake of the Oxford movement's attempts to renew the Church of England and John Henry Newman's celebrated—or scandalous—"going over" to the Catholic Church in 1845, Hopkins's college days were colored by religious ferment. Various letters reflect just how animatedly he and his friends—a number of whom converted or flirted with conversion—debated theological issues. It was Newman, England's most famous convert, who guided Hopkins into the Church and toward the decision, formalized a few years later, to become a Jesuit priest.

Some critics, eager to fix Hopkins in his era, have speculated that he might never have converted had he arrived in Oxford in some other decade. While this may well be true, it's a line of analysis that dismisses Hopkins's own perspective, since he naturally saw his conversion as a response to a divine challenge and invitation ("I cannot fight against God Who calls me to His Church"), all enacted on a scale far grander than mere undergraduate controversy. Readers familiar with critical work on Hopkins will recognize this as a recurrent tension—a disjunction between an ultimately secular outlook and a divine interpretation of events. (It's a clash of viewpoints at the heart of how we choose to regard Hopkins's chaste romantic life. Hopkins's orientation was apparently homosexual, and one might plausibly interpret his flight to the rigors of the Church as an unconscious strategy for avoiding attractions that claimed and unnerved him. But, of course, from Hopkins's angle, any homosexual longings he discerned in himself were varieties of sinful temptation, to be overcome through prayer and perhaps physical mortification.) Not surprisingly, most Hopkins criticism is secular at heart, though without always acknowledging how distorted—how weirdly misguided—Hopkins himself would find all interpretations of a spiritual life that were drawn purely from the outside. For him, a failure to see how divine promptings informed his shaping internal essence—his "inscape," to employ his own term for it—was to miss everything of his life that mattered.

Viewed from the liberal mores of our own era, Hopkins can come across as a bit of a prig. This particular literary revolutionary was, whenever he stepped away from his poet's notebook, a great espouser of orthodoxy. Although he revered Milton's poetry—perhaps the largest single influence on his own—he had trouble forgiving Milton his support for loosening the divorce laws ("he was a very bad man"), and while he sensed profound affinities between himself and Whitman ("I always knew in my heart Walt Whitman's mind to be more like my own than any other man's living"), he avoided Whitman's poetry as the work of a "very great scoundrel." In his letters, he was quick to upbraid friends and family for slippages into inappropriate levity. Where others might have found a tonic irony, he commonly saw corruption, as in this stern admonition of his dear friend Bridges: "And yet let me say, to take no higher ground, that without earnestness there is nothing sound or beautiful in character and that a cynical vein much indulged coarsens everything in us."

When Hopkins's journals first appeared, some critics were pleasantly surprised to find nuggets of humor in them. I can't say I find many. Although he could be amusingly mock-peremptory, Hopkins was a limping humorist at best, as in his few scraps of light verse or a spoof-Irish letter to a sister ("Im intoirely ashamed o meself"). The inchoate roots of much everyday humor—aggression, resentment toward authority, irreverence, sexual tension—were scarcely impulses he meant to foster. Even so, his earnestness may have had an oddly liberating effect: it probably made possible some of his more outlandish experiments with rhyme.

Hopkins regularly concocted rhymes that would seemingly belong more to Thomas Hood or Lord Byron or Ogden Nash than to a grave religious poet who was wrestling with questions of divine justice, spiritual estrangement, the fragility of earthly beauty. How could one possibly employ, as Hopkins did, rhymes like "pain, for the" / "grain for thee" or "ruin" / "crew, in" in a poem that meditates on shipwreck and tragic drowning? Or "boon he on" / "Communion" in a lyric about initiation into the mystical rites of the Church? Only a sensibility radically extracted from conventional trappings of humor, from that entire milieu of snappy banter where everyone's greatest fear is to be made a fool of, could have employed such clownish tools on so grave a poetic mission. In his rhyming, as in so many of his excesses, he was blessedly spared that clarity of sight that would have revealed to him just how near to ludicrous he frequently appeared.

3

Perhaps no other great English poet made it so plain that poetry wasn't the core activity of his life. While William Shakespeare's apparent indifference to the eventual fate of his poems and plays must forever stand as the most puzzling unconcern in our literature, we have in Hopkins's case, unlike Shakespeare's, numerous attestations of how secondary a pursuit poetry was for him.

When he entered the Jesuit novitiate in 1868, Hopkins burned most of his poems and "resolved to write no more, as not belonging to my profession." In a letter to a friend, he explained, "I want to write still and as a priest I very likely can do that too, not so freely as I shd. have liked, e.g. nothing or little in the verse way, but no doubt what wd. best serve the cause of my religion." For seven years he wrote essentially no verse, and when at the age of thirty-one he began again, with the leviathan of "The Wreck of the Deutschland" (his longest poem, and for many people his masterpiece), he did so only at the behest of a superior, who considered the ship's sinking, which included the drowning of five German Franciscan nuns, a fitting subject for commemoration.

Hopkins's letters and journals abound in equally resigned references to the literary sacrifices his vocation imposed. Although one detects sometimes a touch of wistfulness, a hint of remorse at the poems destined to go unwritten, he never faltered in his conviction that he faced more important tasks than stringing lyrical phrases together: "Still, if we care for fine verses how much more for a noble life!"

Later generations of poets who have thrown themselves whole-heartedly into their art, with far less success than Hopkins had, are entitled to feel a little vexed at his example. As if with his left hand, as a mere sideline, Hopkins secured for himself what most poets only dream of—a share of literary immortality. Yet his subordination of poetry to spiritual betterment is far more than a piquant irony: it perfuses the nature of his peculiar accomplishment. Hopkins's genius, as reflected both in his poems and in his letters and journals, depended on this notion that every earthly act served a higher cause.

If poetry isn't an end in itself, but an instrument for elaborating that praise of God which is our chief mortal duty, then it must forever be testing itself against the empirical beauties of creation. Hopkins was constantly touched by a sensation of falling short. The skies he captured in his journals, the flowers he planted in his poems—their real-life models reproached him with their effortless excellences.

This poet who saw each day as "news from God" stalked through the natural world resolutely fixed on noting its often overlooked perfections—the glistening miniatures, the quiet accords and oppositions of hue and shape, the in-between things for which, as in some pre-Adamic state, there were no names:

> Glory be to God for dappled things—
>> For skies of couple-colour as a brinded cow;
>>> For rose-moles all in stipple upon trout that swim;
>> Fresh-firecoal chestnut-falls; finches' wings . . .

He took it as his especial mission to extol whatever was "counter, original, spare, strange." In this he divagated broadly from the tradition of nature verse of his time, and those critics intent on stressing his continuities to Alfred, Lord Tennyson, Wordsworth, Thomas Gray, and others frequently lose sight of what makes Hopkins so compelling: his singularity. (With Hopkins, it takes a while to get past his poems' unrivaled oddities of appearance and delivery, in order to see just how odd he really is.[1])

There's a long and exalted tradition of English nature poetry, extended into the twentieth century by poets like W. H. Auden and Theodore Roethke, in which natural objects rapidly revert to archetypes: trees, flowers, and streams become Trees, Flowers, Streams. But this approach to the universal wasn't Hopkins's; rather, he

---

[1]For a lucid discussion of what Hopkins owed to his predecessors, and where he parted from them, see Virginia Ridley Ellis's *Gerard Manley Hopkins and the Language of Mystery*. (See "Suggestions for Further Reading," p. 185.)

observed of his own temperament that "the effect of studying masterpieces" only made him wish to "do otherwise," and that "more reading would only *refine my singularity*." His approach—support for which he found in the medieval theologian John Duns Scotus—was by way of ever greater particularity and individuation:

> Each mortal thing does one thing and the same:
> Deals out that being indoors each one dwells;
> Selves—goes itself; *myself* it speaks and spells,
> Crying *What I do is me: for that I came.*

This determination to take as his subject Nature's multiplicity, in all its lumpy quiddities, accordingly became fused with a belief that only a new language, a new prosody, was up to the task. The poem in which Hopkins praises creatures "counter, original, spare, strange" is itself a strange animal: a "curtal sonnet," in which both octet and sestet have been truncated to three-quarters their normal length. Even while he embraced that creaky form, the sonnet, Hopkins seems to have been almost constitutionally unable to work in conventional forms conventionally. His nature poetry embodies a conviction that, in rendering the teeming biological world, accuracy demands stylistic extravagance—a notion that likewise would have made sense to Darwin, who as he was preparing to publish *The Origin of Species* remarked in a pair of letters, "Truly the schemes & wonders of nature are illimitable" and "What a wondrous problem it is,—what a play of forces, determining the kinds & proportions of each plant in a square yard of turf!"

Hopkins's relentless search for a tighter fit between the observed and the observation led at times to queer, incongruous analogies, as when, in "God's Grandeur," divine glory is reduced to a sheet of gold foil or to vegetable oil from a press:

The world is charged with the grandeur of God.
It will flame out, like shining from shook foil;
It gathers to a greatness, like the ooze of oil
Crushed. Why do men then now not reck his rod?

When defending himself to Bridges, Hopkins often took refuge in this ideal of accuracy: whatever words or images Bridges happened to question, it would turn out that they held *precisely* the physical traits that Hopkins wanted, and nothing else would quite do the subject justice. Besides, there was gratification to be found in discerning faraway linkages in the divine web, all those half-hidden congruencies that unite the large and the small, the celestial and the humble. Incongruous? What did the word even mean when, as Hopkins insisted, the "only just judge, the only just literary critic, is Christ," to whom all connections are manifest. Hopkins's pursuit of accuracy also bolstered his artistic fearlessness, since on its behalf he was doubly armed: he had a dual sort of faithfulness—both fidelity to the object under his eye and loyalty to a divinely sanctioned task—on his side.

Hopkins's prosody is a complicated business, partly because he experimented in so many different directions, partly because he wasn't always clear or even consistent in his rationales. Here and there, particularly in his letters, he seems determinedly mystical and befuddling, as in his discussion of "outrides," which he defines as an "extra-metrical effect," a phrase not counted when the line is scanned. "It is and it is not part of the meter," he explains—and might almost be a physicist talking about inherently unplaceable subatomic particles. Even prosodic issues, which most other poets would regard as purely mechanical, brimmed with religious significance. As he wrote to Bridges, employing some of the eccentricities of punctuation that flourished in his poetry: "I hold you to be wrong about 'vulgar,' that is obvious or necessary, rhymes. . . . It is nothing that the reader can say / He had to say it, there *was* no other rhyme: you answer / shew me what better I could have said if there had been a million. Hereby, I may tell you, hangs a very profound question treated by Duns Scotus, who shews that freedom is compatible with necessity."

The innovation Hopkins took most pride and interest in was what he called sprung rhythm, a prosodic system in which all unstressed syllables (the "slack," in his designation) are metrically irrelevant: one measures only the number of stresses in a line. The scansion to one of his best-known poems, "Spring and Fall," is a puzzle until one realizes that all lines, despite their variable lengths, contain four stresses:

> Now no matter, child, the name:
> Sorrow's springs are the same.
> Nor mouth had, no nor mind, expressed
> What heart heard of, ghost guessed:
> It is the blight man was born for,
> It is Margaret you mourn for.

Students of prosody may think of this as "pure stress verse" and trace its English origins back to *Beowulf* and Anglo-Saxon. In any case, it wasn't a system that Hopkins claimed to have invented but to have reinvigorated and regularized. Its resurgence might restore English poetry to "the rhythm of prose, that is the native and natural rhythm of speech, the least forced, the most rhetorical and emphatic of all possible rhythms." In a more exultant mood, he declared: "Sprung rhyme gives back to poetry its true soul and self. As poetry is emphatically speech, speech purged of dross like gold in the furnace, so it must have emphatically the essential elements of speech."

What Hopkins might justifiably have claimed to invent, had he wished to, was a poetry in which the music of rhyme is turned inside out. He reversed the roles of external sounds (those falling at the end of a line) and internal sounds (those within the line). At least since Chaucer's day, poets in English have customarily relied on external sounds (usually enhanced by exact rhymes) to create a poem's primary set of echoes, with internal sounds contributing (through assonance, consonance, the occasional chime of an internal rhyme) an enriching accompaniment. Hopkins, on the other hand, "raised the volume" of the internal music to the point where it became primary and the end-rhymes secondary. (Meanwhile in America, Hopkins's contemporary Longfellow was, with less success, turning meter inside out, replacing iambs with trochees in *Hiawatha*.)

Part of the hypnotizing effect of Swinburne's music was its amplifying of internal sounds, largely through rhymes buried within the line, as in "Atalanta and Corydon." But Swinburne hardly took the effect as far as Hopkins. Influenced by his studies of Welsh poetry, which he began after being transferred to St. Beuno's College in North Wales in 1874, Hopkins often set up an unprecedented internal din, whether contemplating Christ's omnipresence:

> Christ minds: Christ's interest, what to avow or amend
>> There, eyes them, heart wants, care haunts, foot follows kind,
>> Their ransom, their rescue, and first, fast, last friend.

or a farmer at his plough:

>> Hard as hurdle arms, with a broth of goldish flue
>> Breathed round; the rack of ribs, the scooped flank; lank
>> Roped-over thigh; knee-nave; and barreled shank . . .

or our fallen earth:

And all is seared with trade, bleared, smeared with toil;
And wears man's smudge, and shares man's smell, the soil
Is bare now . . .

How can a reader possibly be expected to hear that "girlgrace" rhymes with "face," some hundred-plus syllables earlier, in a line like the following (and it *is* all one line): "Winning ways, airs innocent, maiden manners, sweet looks, loose locks, long locks, love-locks, gaygear, going gallant, girlgrace. . . ."

In a second, kindred innovation, Hopkins pioneered the use of what might be called rhyme clusters: big, dense packs of syllables that resound and echo off each other. Typically, he mixed exact rhymes with all sorts of other sonic similarities, as in, above, "wears man's smudge" and "shares man's smell." A phrase like "her fond yellow hornlight" will be immediately followed by "her wild hollow hoarlight"; "Warm-laid grave" yields to "womb-life gray." Traditionally, most English rhyming (with the exception of light verse) has restricted itself to one or two syllables. You might say that Hopkins chose to ring bigger bells.

4

Hopkins's letters and journals often make painful reading. In the end, the solace of his faith was not always sufficient to buoy the temperament of someone who was apparently prone to depression. Toward the end of his short life, he wrote to a friend: "The melancholy I have all my life been subject to has become of late years not indeed more intense in its fits but rather more distributed, constant, and crippling." His counterpart a hundred years later might well have found some relief in medication. For Hopkins, the only "relief" lay in holding himself responsible:

Soon I am afraid I shall be ground down to a state like this last spring's and summer's, when my spirits were so crushed that madness seemed to be making approaches—and nobody was to blame, except myself partly for not managing myself better and contriving a change.

While his correspondence contains instances of greater emotional neediness, perhaps the most affecting moment arises after Bridges disparages Hopkins's creative breakthrough, "The Wreck of the Deutschland." Befuddled by the poem's perplexities and eccentricities, Bridges evidently wrote that he wouldn't read it again for any money. (Because Bridges's correspondence to Hopkins has been lost, what he wrote must be recovered by inference. The wonderful *Letters of Gerard Manley Hopkins to Robert Bridges*[2] offers the reader an opportunity to picture talent engaged in conversation with genius, to imagine Bridges playing Watson to Hopkins's Sherlock Holmes—commonsensically pointing out that this or that poetic effect was impossible, and Hopkins briskly explaining why the seemingly impossible was inevitable.)

Hopkins, who could be quite acerbic, if always affectionately so, toward his friend's shortcomings, responded in a voice of lenity and large-spiritedness: "You say you wd. not for any money read my poem again. Nevertheless I beg you will. Besides money, you know, there is love."

One of the charming aspects of Hopkins's difficulty as a poet is how easily surmounted it was—in his own eyes. He was forever protesting that obscurities and ambiguities all dissolved if his verses were only read with sensitivity to their underlying rhythms. Doubtless, many readers have come to feel, as I have, that it simply isn't always possible, even after long examination of Hopkins's peculiar musical annotations, to hear what their creator had in mind—to detect its auditory inscape. (After Shakespeare, Hopkins is the

---

[2]See "Suggestions for Further Reading," p. 185.

English poet I would most like to hear reading his own verse.) "The Sea and the Skylark" is one of my favorite Hopkins sonnets, but I'm not sure that even his full complement of diacritical annotations allows me to hear it as he would have me hear it:

> On ear and ear two noises too old to end
>   Trench—right, the tide that ramps against the shore;
>   With a flood or a fall, low lull-off or all roar,
> Frequenting there while moon shall wear and wend.

Readers who fear they cannot always catch Hopkins's inner cadences may find it consoling that even scholars who have given him a lifetime of study often disagree on how he hoped to sound or what he meant to say. More consoling still is the realization that, with steady rereading, his lines really do seem warmly to welcome you. Hopkins's landscapes grow more hospitable with time. Their contours show the handsome indwelling harmony of something that has been true to itself. With each new visit to Hopkins country, the rivers run clearer, the birds in the convoluted trees sing with a purer pitch.

CHRONOLOGY OF THE LIFE OF GERARD MANLEY HOPKINS

1844 Born July 28 to Manley and Catherine (Smith) Hopkins in Stratford, Essex, near London's eastern boundary. He will be the eldest of three sisters and five brothers. His father is a marine insurance adjuster, and both parents are cultivated in music and literature. The family religion is High Church Anglican.

1852 The Hopkins family moves to Oakhill, Hampstead. The region is a favorite place for artists and has been visited by Thomas Gainsborough, Sir Joshua Reynolds, George Romney, and John Constable. Ford Madox Brown's paintings, shown in exhibition at Oxford a little over a decade later, will inspire Hopkins with poetic ideas and images.

1854–1863 Hopkins attends Cholmondeley Grammar School in Highgate, north of London. Students are prepared for entrance to Oxford and Cambridge by a classical syllabus with emphasis on the study of Latin and Greek. Hopkins wins five prizes, including the School Poetry Prize for "The Escorial" (1860) and the Governors' Medal for Latin Verse.

1862 Hopkins writes "Il Mystico" and "A Vision of the Mermaids," which reveal the strong influence of John Keats (1795–1821).

1863 Hopkins enters Balliol College, Oxford, in April on a Classical Exhibition scholarship. "Winter with the Gulf Week" had been published in February in *Once a Week*. He begins to keep a journal in which he lists words whose similar sounds seem to him to have associations with meanings, searching out reverberating relationships. He closely observes nature and tries to revisualize what he has seen, as it were, by describing the phenomena in words. He strives both for accuracy of detail and for the poetic image.

It is here that Hopkins meets Robert Bridges (1844–1930), an undergraduate at Corpus Christi College, Oxford. Bridges, who will become an acclaimed poet and in 1913 Poet Laureate, will publish the first edition of Hopkins's complete poems posthumously in 1918.

1864 Influenced by the aesthetics of John Ruskin (1819–1900), English art theorist and critic, Hopkins sketches natural objects as they appear to him empirically rather than through a lens of conventional idealism. The richness and accuracy of detail he tries to convey discipline his attention and lead him into a sacramental sense of the grandeur of nature, i.e., as revelatory of God's presence and glory in the world.

Hopkins comes under the influence of Christina Rossetti (1830–94), a devout High Anglican poet, who is sister to Dante Gabriel Rossetti (1828–82), painter and poet. Christina's mystical passions are greatly influenced by Dante Alighieri (1265–1321) and the *Divine Comedy,* a spiritual odyssey of the passage of sorrow into joy. Christina figures in Hopkins's imagination as a kind of Beatrice of idealized love. Christina's poem "The Convent Threshold" inspires Hopkins to write "A Voice from the World" and "Heaven-Haven."

1865 Hopkins experiences a growing attraction to Roman Catholicism through the influence of his friend Digby Mackworth Dolben, who delights in what were called "mediaeval notions" by their High Church Anglican classmates. Dolben excites the spiritual inclinations buried in Hopkins's nature, and he begins to practice austerities, listing his sins in his diary. "Idleness" and "wasting time," along with self-disgust, are frequent entries. Attracted to the Catholic blessed sacrament of the altar, Hopkins deepens his spiritual practices of prayer, confession, and asceticism this year. Among the many poems he writes are "Easter Communion," "The Alchemist in the City," and "Barnfloor and Winepress," which is published in *The Union Review.*

1866 Hopkins's sacramental confessions within the Anglican Church end in January. His sense of contrast between his personal life and religious life deepens. He writes "The Habit of Perfection," which celebrates a transcendent fulfillment to be gained if the senses are deprived of satisfaction. By July, Hopkins decides he can no longer remain in the Church of England and will become Roman Catholic after he takes his degree.

In August, while on the long vacation from school, Hopkins writes to John Henry Newman about his determination to become Catholic and requests an appointment for a meeting. Newman (1801–90), renowned for his sermons while Anglican vicar of St. Mary's Church, Oxford, himself had joined the Church of Rome in 1845. Newman's *Apologia Pro Vita Sua* (1864), in which he detailed his own spiritual history, is a factor in Hopkins's efforts to resolve his conflict about religious affiliations. Hopkins meets with Newman on September 20, and Newman encourages Hopkins to be received at once into the Church without waiting for the term at Oxford to end. Hopkins's conversion is a cause of great pain to his family and his Anglican friends. Hopkins perseveres in spite of their strong objections and is received into the Roman Church by Newman on October 21.

1867 Hopkins graduates with honors from Oxford in June. He spends the first part of the summer touring northern France. In September he begins teaching classics at Newman's Oratory School in Birmingham. This school has been founded by Newman in 1859 as a Catholic equivalent of an English public school. Hopkins soon finds the lack of private leisure and the incessant duties of school life irksome. At about this time he begins to consider a call to the priesthood.

1868 In April, Hopkins makes a ten-day retreat at the Jesuit Manresa House at Roehampton. He resolves to write no more poetry and to destroy what he has already written as an act of submission to the vocation of the priesthood. In May he applies to the Society of Jesus and is accepted for the Jesuit novitiate. After a summer holiday in Switzerland, he enters the Jesuit Novitiate at Roehampton in September.

Within days after his arrival at Roehampton, Hopkins begins the thirty-day Long Retreat, conducted according to the *Spiritual Exercises* of St. Ignatius of Loyola. It is designed to be a probing and rigorous test of vocation—an ordeal of meditation and penances both physical and mental. Hopkins finds spiritual security in the technique and methodology of the *Exercises,* whose systematic techniques leave little to chance. However, the doctrines of detachment, i.e., to be held to nothing by a tie of affection and to live in a spirit of impersonal obedience like a soldier, are very trying to Hopkins's sensitive nature.

1870 Hopkins makes his vows as a Jesuit on September 8, after two years as a novice. On September 9 he begins a three-year course in philosophy at St. Mary's Hall, Stonyhurst, Lancashire. As a new scholastic, Hopkins wears a Roman collar and a black clerical suit.

Though he finds the northern weather dank and depressing, he continues to record observations of nature in his journal, and these express his innate joy in the natural world.

1872 In August, after exams are finished, Hopkins visits the Isle of Man with a group of seminarians. His excited observations of the architecture of waves and rocks are recorded in his journal in intense and creative images.

About this time Hopkins begins to read the *Oxford Commentary* of John Duns Scotus (c. 1266–1308) on the *Sentences* of Peter Lombard (c. 1095–1160). Duns Scotus, a Scottish Franciscan, considered the Incarnation a supreme manifestation of God's love that was intended by Him from all eternity regardless of man's need for redemption from the Fall. In addition, Hopkins finds that Scotus's emphasis on the unique individuality of each natural object as it yields its specific pattern to the persistent effort of moving in perception from the less distinct to the more distinct features of the thing (its *haecceitas,* or "thisness") is a doctrinal correlative of his own theory of "inscape" and "pitch." Hopkins's love for the inscapes of nature and his sense that all beauty dwells ultimately in God are sanctioned by Scotus's view that God's participation in all nature through the Incarnation is consummated in the person of Christ.

1873 In September, Hopkins begins teaching rhetoric at Roehampton. This assignment is a year of "rest" before he proceeds to his theology training. During this time he is able to visit museums, galleries, and exhibitions, making careful notes in his journal on the paintings and sculptures, especially oil landscapes. He is also able to renew his friendship with Robert Bridges, which had suffered an interruption for over two years because of Bridges's antagonism toward Catholicism and, particularly, the Jesuits.

1874 In August, Hopkins is assigned to St. Beuno's College in North Wales for his Jesuit theology studies, a four-year course. The academics are intense and time-consuming, leaving him little leisure for correspondence or journal writing. In September, Hopkins receives the minor clerical orders as a step toward his ordination as a priest.

From the beginning Hopkins is drawn to the musical beauty of the Welsh language, and he longs to become proficient in this tongue. He takes lessons for a brief period but lacks the time to give to the study. However, he learns enough so that later he will incorporate some Welsh poetic techniques into his own compositions.

Soon after his arrival at St. Beuno's, Hopkins visits the healing waters of St. Winefride's Well, where he bathes. Winefride's story dates to the twelfth century and recounts her beheading at the hand of a chieftain who killed her when she resisted his advances. A spring welled up where her severed head had touched the ground. The alleged cures at the well continued over the centuries, and Hopkins becomes devoted to the site, where he feels that God's glory is manifested through nature for man's well-being.

1875 In December a ship carrying some nuns exiled from Prussia founders on a sandbank in the mouth of the Thames during a heavy snowstorm. Hopkins is keenly aware of the persecution of Catholics in Protestant Europe, and the English Province of the Jesuits has offered sanctuary to priests who have been expelled from Spain, Rome, and Germany. The five Franciscan nuns are on their way to America when the shipping disaster occurs. Hopkins finds himself mightily stirred by the report that the chief sister, a tall, gaunt woman, was heard crying out, "O Christ, come quickly!" as inescapable death came nearer and nearer in the pounding seas. Father James Jones, rector of St. Beuno's College, suggests to Hopkins that he write a poem commemorating the event. Hopkins then breaks seven years of poetic silence to write what will come to endure as his masterpiece, "The Wreck of the Deutschland."

The first part of the poem is subjective, an account of Hopkins's personal anguish and suffering over his conversion, and the second part concerns the plight of the nuns on the doomed ship. Both "wrecks" exemplify the action of God in the life of the human being by which one is invited to choose God, when put to the ultimate stress, by offering up existence itself to Him. The poem is a two-part ode of thirty-five eight-line stanzas in which Hopkins's techniques of sprung rhythm, alliteration, and parallelism are fully utilized. It also incorporates his sense of the presence of God in the terrifying sublimity of the power of nature in the ocean storm, a presence that invites his prostration and submission. "Thou mastering me / God! giver of breath and bread;" as the opening words of the poem testify.

1876 Hopkins completes "The Wreck of the Deutschland" in the spring and submits it to *The Month,* a Jesuit journal, for publication in July. It is ultimately rejected. Hopkins is deeply and irrevocably hurt by this refusal. However, "The Silver Jubilee," an anniversary poem in honor of James Brown, first bishop of North Wales since the Catholic hierarchy was restored to Britain in 1850, is published to some acclaim. He also writes "Cywydd," "Moonrise," and "The Woodlark."

1877 Between February and September, while worrying over his final exams in moral theology, Hopkins writes his great nature poems, including "God's Grandeur," "The Starlight Night," "As kingfishers catch fire," "Spring," "The Windhover," and "Pied Beauty." On July 22, Hopkins is examined in dogmatic theology, but his Scotist leanings clash with the Thomism of his examiners, and his grades are low. He is not accepted for the fourth year of theology at St. Beuno's. This will ultimately work to check advancement in his career as a Jesuit.

Hopkins is ordained a priest on September 23. His family is not in attendance. He is then posted to Mount St. Mary's College in Chesterfield as assistant to the parish priest and as a teacher of classics in the boys' school.

1878 Pope Pius IX dies and is succeeded by Pope Leo XIII, a onetime pupil of the Jesuits. On March 24, the HMS *Eurydice* sinks in a squall off the southeast coast of the Isle of Wight, with only two survivors out of 368 aboard. Hopkins writes "The Loss of the Eurydice," a poem shorter than his long ode "The Wreck of the Deutschland," and in a more narrative form. He incorporates into this composition many of the criticisms and suggestions Robert Bridges had made to him about the "Deutschland." Bridges is very complimentary about the newer poem, but Hopkins again receives a rejection from *The Month* when he submits it for publication.

In April, Hopkins is sent to Stonyhurst College to coach students preparing for degrees at the University of London. There he writes "The May Magnificat" in honor of the Virgin Mary.

In June, Hopkins writes to Canon R. W. Dixon, a Church of England pastor whom Hopkins had known at Highgate School years before. Dixon is a little-known poet much appreciated by Hopkins. A friendship begins between them. In July, Hopkins is sent to London to serve at the Jesuit church of Farm Street, Mayfair. His friend Robert Bridges attends Mass to hear him preach but remains critical of the Catholic Church. Hopkins urges Dixon and Bridges to read each other's poems. In December, Hopkins's assignment is again changed, and he goes to St. Aloysius Church, at Oxford, where he does parish work. He is not successful here as a preacher, misjudging, as he so often has in the past, idioms and subjects congenial to his congregation's tastes and spirits.

1879 During his stay at St. Aloysius, Hopkins produces a number of poems, among them "Duns Scotus's Oxford," "Binsey Poplars," and "Henry Purcell." In October he is moved to Bedford Leigh, near Manchester, a small industrial town. Here he finds a congenial match between his own spiritual focus and the devotion of the local people. It is his happiest period as a priest. After Christmas, Hopkins is sent to St. Francis Xavier in Liverpool, a large, busy urban parish. Here he tries a more elaborate approach to his sermon topics and fails notably to interest or inspire his listeners. His health is affected by the stress, and he suffers from vomiting and diarrhea.

1880 Hopkins composes "Felix Randal" and "Spring and Fall." The latter will become one of his most popular poems.

1881 In April, Hopkins sends three sonnets to Hall Caine after Dixon has recommended Hopkins's work to Caine, who is preparing an anthology. However, none of the poems is published in it.

In August, Hopkins is sent to St. Joseph's parish in Glasgow as a temporary substitute. He finds the assignment congenial though busy, giving him little time to write either poems or letters. As his stay comes to an end, he makes a brief visit to the outskirts of the Highlands and then writes "Inversnaid," inspired by William Wordsworth's poem "To a Highland Girl." Wordsworth (1770–1850), the great Romantic innovator who took delight in the powers of perceptual experience, sought to re-create them in poetry "as emotion recollected in tranquility."

In October, Hopkins begins his tertianship, or noviceship,[3] at Manresa House, Roehampton, in preparation for his final vows as a Jesuit. He enters the Long Retreat on November 7. Again his sense of conflict between his call to the priesthood and the desire to write rises up in his soul. He struggles to resign himself to the hidden life ordained by his vows, trying to convince himself that it is altogether holier to remain unknown than to acquire fame, which could be a temptation to vainglory. He has scruples over his preoccupation with writing poetry and letters of criticism to friends like Dixon and Bridges, thinking that God will judge him severely for wasting his time as a priest with such matters.

At the start of Lent in March, Hopkins is sent to St. Wilfrid's, Preston, Lancashire, for parish work; then, in April, to St. Elizabeth's, in Richmond, Surrey; and finally, back to Manresa in May. Near the end of his ten-month tertianship, Hopkins writes a commentary on the *Spiritual Exercises* of St. Ignatius of Loyola. He pronounces his final vows during Mass on the feast of the Assumption, August 15.

1882 Hopkins begins his assignment as a teacher of classics at Stoneyhurst College in Lancashire with a mission to prepare students for the London University Intermediate and B.A. exams. He composes "The Leaden Echo and the Golden Echo," which is suggestive

---

[3]A period of preparation for final vows, which are perpetually binding. Like the noviceship, it is a time of withdrawal from the world for instruction in the truths of religion and exercises in prayer. Tertianship in the Society of Jesus comes for priests after ordination but before the solemn profession of the vows of poverty, chastity, and obedience. It includes a thirty-day retreat based on the *Spiritual Exercises* of St. Ignatius of Loyola, an intense physical and mental ordeal in which the retreatants are trained and disciplined to commit to the Ignatian ideals of complete conformity to God's will, detachment from personal tastes and desires, and the obedience of a soldier to his commanding officer (in this case the religious superior). A Jesuit is trained to conquer himself, regulate his life, and avoid decisions made under the influence of disordered passions.

of the influence of Walt Whitman (1819–92). The American's blend of realism, the lyricism of simple speech, and the cosmic "I" that identifies with all the elements of the universe appeals to Hopkins, though he thought the man himself to be a scoundrel. Hopkins writes "Ribblesdale," a description of the Lancashire landscape.

1883 In May, the month traditionally devoted to Mary, he writes "The Blessed Virgin compared to the Air we Breathe." He attempts, as he has several times in the past, to compose music. Hopkins acquires a reputation for eccentric ways. To distract a young boy wandering the playing grounds while suffering from a toothache, he takes off his cassock and shinnies up a goalpost. Another time he chases after a pet monkey that had escaped to the roof and coaxes it back from its perch on a narrow and dangerous ledge.

Hopkins's sad, tired spirits are revived by a four-day visit to Stoneyhurst by Coventry Patmore (1823–96), whose poems Hopkins admires. After Patmore's visit, Hopkins travels to London, where he is visited by Bridges, and then joins his parents and cousin Kate in Holland for the last week in August.

Hopkins is reappointed to Stoneyhurst for the autumn term. His intellectual life is enlivened by correspondence with Patmore, which grows out of Patmore's gift to him of four volumes of his poetry. This allows Hopkins to exercise his great gift of careful critical literary analysis.

1884 In February, Hopkins becomes a Fellow of the Royal University of Ireland and Professor of Greek at University College, Dublin. The university, scene of John Henry Newman's bitter disappointment and defeat by the Irish bishops, who opposed his ideas about what a great university should be (see Newman's *The Idea of a Uni-*

versity), is now an institution in decline and dilapidation. The Jesuits have been put in charge. Hopkins is soon depressed and overwhelmed by the onerous examination schedule and his own lack of success as a lecturer. He refers to the examination in his letters as periods of "illness" that leave him exhausted. He feels altogether that he has become "Fortune's football." In October he begins to compose "St. Winefred's Well" and "Spelt from Sybil's Leaves."

1885 Hopkins's sense of desolation deepens. He cannot acclimate himself to Ireland: the continual damp of the climate, the diffidence of his students, the onerous tasks of examination and correction, the lack of educational standards and any sense of European culture. He begins to suffer headaches and falls into despondency. He is depressed by his separation from his family and England, and by the uncongeniality of Irish Catholicism, which he perceives to be in contention with legitimate authority. In this spirit of alienation, he composes his "Sonnets of Desolation," including: "To seem the stranger," "I wake and feel," "Not, I'll not, carrion comfort," "No worst, there is none," and "To what serves Mortal Beauty."

1886 Hopkins finds some relief from his loneliness in friendship with the McCabe family in nearby Donnybrook. Dr. McCabe and his wife welcome Hopkins into their home, where he enjoys the company of five children and the general good humor of the household. He takes a holiday in England in the spring and is able to meet with Alexander Baillie, an authority on Egypt and Greek, and Bridges, as well as to stay at his family home.

Hopkins turns to musical composition again and this time submits a tune to Sir Robert Stewart, who holds two chairs in Dublin, at the Royal Irish Academy of Music and Dublin University. Stewart picks up right away on Hopkins's trait of defending himself voluminously against criticism and tells him it is better for him to remain in his "happy dreams of perfectibility." Criticizing the musical faults in his composition, he exposes Hopkins's lack of education in musical grammar and convention.

In September, Hopkins vacations with his friend Robert Curtis in Wales. His spirits are improved by the rest and diversion. He completes "Spelt from Sibyl's Leaves," translates "Songs from Shakespeare," and writes "On the Portrait of Two Beautiful Young People."

1887 Hopkins puts in his journal on February 17: "I shall have been three years in Ireland, three hard wearying wasting wasted years." Increasing civil rebellion causes him to accept the idea of home rule for the Irish, but he despairs of them ever being capable of civil allegiance to any existing government. He writes "Harry Ploughman" and "Tom's Garland," both of which reflect his social theories. He is introduced to Katherine Tynan (1859–1931), a Dublin poet and novelist who is a friend of the young Anglo-Irish poet William Butler Yeats (1865–1939). Hopkins enjoys his occasional visits with her literary circle of friends.

1888 Hopkins composes "That Nature is a Heraclitean Fire," a poem that cancels the elation over creation expressed in its opening lines with a stark submission to the promise of fulfillment only in the hope of the Resurrection. He also writes "In honour of St. Alphonsus Rodriguez" in recognition of the canonization of the Jesuit lay brother who lived a life of total obscurity as a college porter. His weariness and depression deepen.

1889 Hopkins begins the year on retreat at the Irish novitiate of Tullabeg. He has now been a member of the Society of Jesus for twenty years. He feels his life is wretched, that his weakness has prevented him from accomplishing anything lasting. On March 17, Saint Patrick's Day, he writes the poem "Thou art indeed just, Lord," in which he identifies with the travails of the prophet Jeremiah. In April he writes "The shepherd's brow," and finally his last poem, "To R.B.," which he sends to his friend Bridges with a letter. Robert Bridges is to be his poetic executor.

Hopkins then falls ill with a fever. He had contracted a virulent form of typhoid. Peritonitis sets in during the first days of June, and he dies on June 8.

Gerard Manley Hopkins is buried on the north side of Dublin in Prospect Cemetery, Glasnevin.

1918 Robert Bridges, now Poet Laureate of England, edits the first edition of Hopkins's *Poems,* which is published in London.

Poetry

HEAVEN-HAVEN

(a nun takes the veil)

I have desired to go
    Where springs not fail,
To fields where flies no sharp and sided hail
    And a few lilies blow.

And I have asked to be
    Where no storms come,
Where the green swell is in the havens dumb,
    And out of the swing of the sea.

THE HABIT OF PERFECTION

Elected Silence, sing to me
And beat upon my whorlèd ear,
Pipe me to pastures still and be
The music that I care to hear.

Shape nothing, lips; be lovely-dumb:
It is the shut, the curfew sent
From there where all surrenders come
Which only makes you eloquent.

Be shellèd, eyes, with double dark
And find the uncreated light:
This ruck and reel which you remark
Coils, keeps, and teases simple sight.

Palate, the hutch of tasty lust,
Desire not to be rinsed with wine:
The can must be so sweet, the crust
So fresh that come in fasts divine!

Nostrils, your careless breath that spend
Upon the stir and keep of pride,
What relish shall the censers send
Along the sanctuary side!

O feel-of-primrose hands, O feet
That want the yield of plushy sward,
But you shall walk the golden street
And you unhouse and house the Lord.

And, Poverty, be thou the bride
And now the marriage feast begun,
And lily-coloured clothes provide
Your spouse not laboured-at nor spun.

NONDUM [4]
"Verily Thou art a God that hidest Thyself."
ISAIAH 45:15

God, though to Thee our psalm we raise
No answering voice comes from the skies;
To Thee the trembling sinner prays
But no forgiving voice replies;

[4]From Latin, "not yet."

[4]

Our prayer seems lost in desert ways,
Our hymn in the vast silence dies.

We see the glories of the earth
But not the hand that wrought them all:
Night to a myriad worlds gives birth,
Yet like a lighted empty hall
Where stands no host at door or hearth
Vacant creation's lamps appal.

We guess; we clothe Thee, unseen King,
With attributes we deem are meet;
Each in his own imagining
Sets up a shadow in Thy seat;
Yet know not how our gifts to bring,
Where seek Thee with unsandalled feet.

And still th'unbroken silence broods
While ages and while aeons run,
As erst upon chaotic floods
The Spirit hovered ere the sun
Had called the seasons' changeful moods
And life's first germs from death had won.

And still th'abysses infinite
Surround the peak from which we gaze.
Deep calls to deep, and blackest night
Giddies the soul with blinding daze
That dares to cast its searching sight
On being's dread and vacant maze.

And Thou art silent, whilst Thy world
Contends about its many creeds
And hosts confront with flags unfurled
And zeal is flushed and pity bleeds
And truth is heard, with tears impearled,
A moaning voice among the reeds.

My hand upon my lips I lay;
The breast's desponding sob I quell;
I move along life's tomb-decked way
And listen to the passing bell
Summoning men from speechless day
To death's more silent, darker spell.

Oh! till Thou givest that sense beyond,
To shew Thee that Thou art, and near,
Let patience with her chastening wand
Dispel the doubt and dry the tear;
And lead me child-like by the hand
If still in darkness not in fear.

Speak! whisper to my watching heart
One word—as when a mother speaks
Soft, when she sees her infant start,
Till dimpled joy steals o'er its cheeks.
Then, to behold Thee as Thou art,
I'll wait till morn eternal breaks.

ORATIO PATRIS CONDREN: O JESU VIVENS IN MARIA

Jesu that dost in Mary dwell,
Be in thy servants' hearts as well,
In the spirit of thy holiness,
In the fulness of thy force and stress,
In the very ways that thy life goes
And virtues that thy pattern shows,
In the sharing of thy mysteries;
And every power in us that is
Against thy power put under feet
In the Holy Ghost the Paraclete
    To the glory of the Father. Amen.

S. THOMAE AQUINATIS
RHYTHMUS AD SS. SACRAMENTUM
"Adoro te supplex, latens deitas"

Godhead, I adore thee fast in hiding; thou
God in these bare shapes, poor shadows, darkling now:
See, Lord, at thy service low lies here a heart
Lost, all lost in wonder at the God thou art.

Seeing, touching, tasting are in thee deceived;
How says trusty hearing? that shall be believed:
What God's Son has told me, take for truth I do;
Truth himself speaks truly or there's nothing true.

On the cross thy godhead made no sign to men;
Here thy very manhood steals from human ken:

Both are my confession, both are my belief,
And I pray the prayer of the dying thief.

I am not like Thomas, wounds I cannot see,
But can plainly call thee Lord and God as he:
This faith each day deeper be my holding of,
Daily make me harder hope and dearer love.

O thou our reminder of Christ crucified,
Living Bread the life of us for whom he died,
Lend this life to me then: feed and feast my mind,
There be thou the sweetness man was meant to find.

Like what tender tales tell of the Pelican;
Bathe me, Jesu Lord, in what thy bosom ran—
Blood that but one drop of has the worth to win
All the world forgiveness of its world of sin.

Jesu whom I look at veilèd here below,
I beseech thee send me what I thirst for so,
Some day to gaze on thee face to face in light
And be blest for ever with thy glory's sight.

The Wreck of the Deutschland
Dec. 6, 7, 1875

to the happy memory of five Franciscan nuns,
exiles by the Falck Laws, drowned between
midnight and morning of December 7.

Part the first

Thou mastering me
God! giver of breath and bread;
World's strand, sway of the sea;
Lord of living and dead;
Thou hast bound bones and veins in me, fastened me flesh,
And after it álmost únmade, what with dread,
Thy doing: and dost thou touch me afresh?
Over again I feel thy finger and find theé.

2

I did say yes
O at lightning and lashed rod;
Thou heardst me truer than tongue confess
Thy terror, O Christ, O God;
Thou knowest the walls, altar and hour and night:
The swoon of a heart that the sweep and the hurl of thee trod
Hard down with a horror of height:
And the midriff astrain with leaning of, laced with fire of stress.

3

The frown of his face
Before me, the hurtle of hell
Behind, where, where was a, where was a place?

I whirled out wings that spell
And fled with a fling of the heart to the heart of the Host.
My heart, but you were dovewinged, I can tell,
    Carrier-witted, I am bold to boast,
To flash from the flame to the flame then, tower from the grace to the
        grace.

4

    I am sóft sift
        In an hourglass—at the wall
    Fast, but mined with a motion, a drift,
        And it crowds and it combs to the fall;
    I steady as a water in a well, to a poise, to a pane,
        But roped with, always, all the way down from the tall
            Fells or flanks of the voel, a vein
Of the gospel proffer, a pressure, a principle, Christ's gift.

5

    I kiss my hand
        To the stars, lovely-asunder
    Starlight, wafting him out of it; and
        Glow, glory in thunder;
    Kiss my hand to the dappled-with-damson west:
        Since, though he is under the world's splendour and wonder,
            His mystery must be instressed, stressed;
For I greet him the days I meet him, and bless when I understand.

6

    Not out of his bliss
        Springs the stress felt
    Nor first from heaven (and few know this)
        Swings the stroke dealt—

Stroke and a stress that stars and storms deliver,
That guilt is hushed by, hearts are flushed by and melt—
But it rides time like riding a river
(And here the faithful waver, the faithless fable and miss.)

7

It dates from day
Of his going in Galilee;
Warm-laid grave of a womb-life grey;
Manger, maiden's knee;
The dense and the driven Passion, and frightful sweat;
Thence the discharge of it, there its swelling to be,
Though felt before, though in high flood yet—
What none would have known of it, only the heart, being hard at bay,

8

Is out with it! Oh,
We lash with the best or worst
Word last! How a lush-kept plush-capped sloe
Will, mouthed to flesh-burst,
Gush!—flush the man, the being with it, sour or sweet,
Brim, in a flash, full!—Hither then, last or first,
To hero of Calvary, Christ's, feet—
Never ask if meaning it, wanting it, warned of it—men go.

9

Be adored among men,
God, three-numberèd form;
Wring thy rebel, dogged in den,
Man's malice, with wrecking and storm.
Beyond saying sweet, past telling of tongue,
Thou art lightning and love, I found it, a winter and warm;

Father and fondler of heart thou hast wrung;
Hast thy dark descending and most art merciful then.

10

With an anvil-ding
And with fire in him forge thy will
Or rather, rather then, stealing as Spring
Through him, melt him but master him still:
Whether át ónce, as once at a crash Paul,
Or as Austin,[5] a lingering-out sweet skill,
Make mercy in all of us, out of us all
Mastery, but be adored, but be adored King.

Part the second

11

"Some find me a sword; some
The flange and the rail; flame,
Fang, or flood" goes Death on drum,
And storms bugle his fame.
But wé dréam we are rooted in earth—Dust!
Flesh falls within sight of us: we, though our flower the same,
Wave with the meadow, forget that there must
The sour scythe cringe, and the blear share come.

12

On Saturday sailed from Bremen,
American-outward-bound,
Take settler and seamen, tell men with women,
Two hundred souls in the round—
O Father, not under thy feathers nor ever as guessing

[5]St. Augustine of Hippo (345–430).

The goal was a shoal, of a fourth the doom to be drowned;
 Yet díd the dark side of the bay of thy blessing
Not vault them, the million of rounds of thy mercy not reeve even
  them in?

13

 Into the snows she sweeps,
  Hurling the Haven behind,
 The Deutschland, on Sunday; and so the sky keeps,
  For the infinite air is unkind,
And the sea flint-flake, black-backed in the regular blow,
Sitting Eastnortheast, in cursed quarter, the wind;
 Wiry and white-fiery and whírlwind-swivellèd snow
Spins to the widow-making unchilding unfathering deeps.

14

 She drove in the dark to leeward,
  She struck—not a reef or a rock
 But the combs of a smother of sand: night drew her
  Dead to the Kentish Knock;
And she beat the bank down with her bows and the ride of her
  keel;
The breakers rolled on her beam with ruinous shock;
 And canvass and compass, the whorl and the wheel
Idle for ever to waft her or wind her with, these she endured.

15

 Hope had grown grey hairs,
  Hope had mourning on,
 Trenched with tears, carved with cares,
  Hope was twelve hours gone;
And frightful a nightfall folded rueful a day

Nor rescue, only rocket and lightship, shone,
    And lives at last were washing away:
To the shrouds they took,—they shook in the hurling and horrible airs.

16

    One stirred from the rigging to save
    The wild woman-kind below,
        With a rope's end round the man, handy and brave—
        He was pitched to his death at a blow,
For all his dreadnought breast and braids of thew:
    They could tell him for hours, dandled the to and fro
        Through the cobbled foam-fleece. What could he do
With the burl of the fountains of air, buck and the flood of the wave?

17

    They fought with God's cold—
    And they could not and fell to the deck
        (Crushed them) or water (and drowned them) or rolled
        With the sea-romp over the wreck.
Night roared, with the heart-break hearing a heart-broke
            rabble,
    The woman's wailing, the crying of child without check—
        Till a lioness arose breasting the babble,
A prophetess towered in the tumult, a virginal tongue told.

18

    Ah, touched in your bower of bone
    Are you! turned for an exquisite smart,
        Have you! make words break from me here all alone,
        Do you!—mother of being in me, heart.
O unteachably after evil, but uttering truth,
    Why, tears! is it? tears; such a melting, a madrigal start!

Never-eldering revel and river of youth,
What can it be, this glee? the good you have there of your own?

19

Sister, a sister calling
A master, her master and mine!—
And the inboard seas run swirling and hawling;
The rash smart sloggering brine
Blinds her; but shé that weather sees óne thing, one;
Has óne fetch ín her: she rears herself to divine
Ears, and the call of the tall nun
To the men in the tops and the tackle rode over the storm's brawling.

20

She was first of a five and came
of a coifèd sisterhood.
(O Deutschland, double a desperate name!
O world wide of its good!
But Gertrude, lily, and Luther, are two of a town,
Christ's lily and beast of the waste wood:
From life's dawn it is drawn down,
Abel is Cain's brother and breasts they have sucked the same.)

21

Loathed for a love men knew in them,
Banned by the land of their birth,
Rhine refused them, Thames would ruin them;
Surf, snow, river and earth
Gnashed: but thou art above, thou Orion of light;
Thy unchancelling poising palms were weighing the worth,

Thou martyr-master: in thý sight
Storm flakes were scroll-leaved flowers, lily showers—sweet heaven
was astrew in them.

22

Five! the finding and sake
And cipher of suffering Christ.
Mark, the mark is of man's make
And the word of it Sacrificed.
But he scores it in scarlet himself on his own bespoken,
Before-time-taken, dearest prizèd and priced—
Stigma, signal, cinquefoil token
For lettering of the lamb's fleece, ruddying of the rose-flake.

23

Joy fall to thee, father Francis,
Drawn to the Life that died;
With the gnarls of the nails in thee, niche of the lance, his
Lovescape crucified
And seal of his seraph-arrival! and these thy daughters
And five-livèd and leavèd favour and pride,
Are sisterly sealed in wild waters,
To bathe in his fall-gold mercies, to breathe in his all-fire glances.

24

Away in the loveable west,
On a pastoral forehead of Wales,
I was under a roof here, I was at rest,
And they the prey of the gales;
She to the black-about air, to the breaker, the thickly
Falling flakes, to the throng that catches and quails

Was calling "O Christ, Christ, come quickly":
The cross to her she calls Christ to her, christens her wild-worst Best.

25

The majesty! what did she mean?
Breathe, arch and original Breath.
Is it lóve in her of the béing as her lóver had béen?
Breathe, body of lovely Death.
They were else-minded then, altogether, the men
Woke thee with a *We are périshing* in the wéather of Gennésaréth.
Or ís it that she cried for the crown then,
The keener to come at the comfort for feeling the combating keen?

26

For how to the heart's cheering
The down-dugged ground-hugged grey
Hovers off, the jay-blue heavens appearing
Of pied and peeled May!
Blue-beating and hoary-glow height; or night, still higher,
With belled fire and the moth-soft Milky Way,
What by your measure is the heaven of desire,
The treasure never eyesight got, nor was ever guessed what for the
hearing?

27

Nó, but it was nót these.
The jading and jar of the cart,
Time's tásking, it is fathers that asking for ease
Of the sodden-with-its-sorrowing heart,
Not danger, electrical horror; then further it finds
The appealing of the Passion is tenderer in prayer apart:

Other, I gather, in measure her mind's
Burden, in wind's burly and beat of endragonèd seas.

28

But how shall I . . . make me room there:
Reach me a . . . Fancy, come faster—
Strike you the sight of it? look at it loom there,
Thing that she . . . There then! the Master,
Ipse, the only one, Christ, King, Head:
He was to cure the extremity where he had cast her;
Do, deal, lord it with living and dead;
Let him ride, her pride, in his triumph, despatch and have done with
his doom there.

29

Ah! there was a heart right!
There was single eye!
Read the unshapeable shock night
And knew the who and the why;
Wording it how but by him that present and past,
Heaven and earth are word of, worded by?—
The Simon Peter of a soul! to the blast
Tárpéïan-fast, but a blown beacon of light.

30

Jesu, heart's light,
Jesu, maid's son,
What was the feast followed the night
Thou hadst glory of this nun?—
Féast of the óne wóman withóut stáin.
For so conceivèd, so to conceive thee is done;

But here was heart-throe, birth of a brain,
Word, that heard and kept thee and uttered thee óutríght.

31

Well, shé has thée for the pain, for the
Patience; but pity of the rest of them!
Heart, go and bleed at a bitterer vein for the
Comfortless unconfessed of them—
No not uncomforted: lovely-felicitious Providence
Fínger of a ténder of, O of a féathery délicacy, the bréast of the
Maiden could obey so, be a bell to, ring óf it, and
Startle the poor sheep back! is the shipwrack then a harvest, does
tempest carry the grain for thee?

32

I admire thee, master of the tides,
Of the Yore-flood, of the year's fall;
The recurb and the recovery of the gulf's sides,
The girth of it and the wharf of it and the wall;
Stanching, quenching ocean of a motionable mind;
Ground of being, and granite of it; pást áll
Grásp Gód, thróned behínd
Death with a sovereignty that heeds but hides, bodes but abides;

33

With a mercy that outrides
The all of water, an ark
For the listener; for the lingerer with a love glides
Lower than death and the dark;
A vein for the visiting of the past-prayer, pent in prison,
The-last-breath penitent spirits—the uttermost mark

Our passion-plungèd giant risen,
The Christ of the Father compassionate, fetched in the storm of his
    strides.

34

Now burn, new born to the world,
    Double-naturèd name,
The heaven-flung, heart-fleshed, maiden-furled
    Miracle-in-Mary-of-flame,
Mid-numberèd he in three of the thunder-throne!
Not a dooms-day dazzle in his coming nor dark as he came;
    Kind, but royally reclaiming his own;
A released shówer, let flásh to the shíre, not a líghtning of fíre
    hard-húrled.

35

Dame, at our door
    Drówned, and among oúr shóals,
Remember us in the roads, the heaven-haven of the
    reward:
    Our Kíng back, Oh, upon Énglish sóuls!
Let him easter in us, be a dayspring to the dimness of us, be a
    crimson-cresseted east,
More brightening her, rare-dear Britain, as his reign rolls,
    Pride, rose, prince, hero of us, high-priest,
Our héarts' charity's héarth's fire, our thóughts' chivalry's thróng's
    Lórd.

God's Grandeur

The world is charged with the grandeur of God.
   It will flame out, like shining from shook foil;
   It gathers to a greatness, like the ooze of oil
Crushed. Why do men then now not reck his rod?
Generations have trod, have trod, have trod;
   And all is seared with trade; bleared, smeared with toil;
   And wears man's smudge and shares man's smell: the soil
Is bare now, nor can foot feel, being shod.

And, for all this, nature is never spent;
   There lives the dearest freshness deep down things;
And though the last lights off the black West went
   Oh, morning, at the brown brink eastwards, springs—
Because the Holy Ghost over the bent
   World broods with warm breast and with ah! bright wings.

The Starlight Night

Look at the stars! look, look up at the skies!
   O look at all the fire-folk sitting in the air!
   The bright boroughs, the circle-citadels there!
Down in dim woods the diamond delves! the elves'-eyes!
The grey lawns cold where gold, where quickgold lies!
   Wind-beat whitebeam! airy abeles set on a flare!
   Flake-doves sent floating forth at a farmyard scare!—
Ah well! it is all a purchase, all is a prize.

Buy then! bid then!—What?—Prayer, patience, alms, vows.
Look, look: a May-mess, like on orchard boughs!
  Look! March-bloom, like on mealed-with-yellow sallows!
These are indeed the barn; withindoors house
The shocks. This piece-bright paling shuts the spouse
  Christ home, Christ and his mother and all his hallows.

THE SEA AND THE SKYLARK

On ear and ear two noises too old to end
  Trench—right, the tide that ramps against the shore;
  With a flood or a fall, low lull-off or all roar,
Frequenting there while moon shall wear and wend.

Left hand, off land, I hear the lark ascend,
  His rash-fresh re-winded new-skeinèd score
  In crisps of curl off wild winch whirl, and pour
And pelt music, till none's to spill nor spend.

How these two shame this shallow and frail town!
  How ring right out our sordid turbid time,
Being pure! We, life's pride and cared-for crown,

  Have lost that cheer and charm of earth's past prime:
Our make and making break, are breaking, down
  To man's last dust, drain fast towards man's first slime.

"As kingfishers catch fire"

As kingfishers catch fire, dragonflies draw flame;
    As tumbled over rim in roundy wells
    Stones ring; like each tucked string tells, each hung bell's
Bow swung finds tongue to fling out broad its name;
Each mortal thing does one thing and the same:
    Deals out that being indoors each one dwells;
    Selves—goes its self; *myself* it speaks and spells,
Crying *What I do is me: for that I came.*

I say more: the just man justices;
    Keeps grace: that keeps all his goings graces;
Acts in God's eye what in God's eye he is—
    Christ. For Christ plays in ten thousand places,
Lovely in limbs, and lovely in eyes not his
    To the Father through the features of men's faces.

Spring

Nothing is so beautiful as Spring—
    When weeds, in wheels, shoot long and lovely and lush;
    Thrush's eggs look little low heavens, and thrush
Through the echoing timber does so rinse and wring

The ear, it strikes like lightnings to hear him sing;
    The glassy peartree leaves and blooms, they brush
    The descending blue; that blue is all in a rush
With richness; the racing lambs too have fair their fling.

What is all this juice and all this joy?
    A strain of the earth's sweet being in the beginning
In Eden garden.—Have, get before it cloy,

    Before it cloud, Christ, lord, and sour with sinning,
Innocent mind and Mayday in girl and boy,
    Most, O maid's child, thy choice and worthy the winning.

THE WINDHOVER:
to Christ our Lord

I caught this morning morning's minion, king-
    dom of daylight's dauphin, dapple-dáwn-drawn Falcon, in his
        riding
Of the rólling level úndernéath him steady áir, and stríding
High there, how he rung upon the rein of a wimpling wing
In his ecstasy! then off, off forth on swing,
    As a skate's heel sweeps smooth on a bow-bend: the hurl and
        gliding
Rebuffed the big wind. My heart in hiding
Stirred for a bird,—the achieve of, the mastery of the thing!

Brute beauty and valour and act, oh, air, pride, plume, here
    Buckle! AND the fire that breaks from thee then, a billion
Times told lovelier, more dangerous, O my chevalier!

    No wónder of it: shéer plód makes plóugh down síllion
Shine, and blue-bleak embers, ah my dear,
    Fall, gáll themsélves, and gásh góld-vermílion.

PIED BEAUTY

Glory be to God for dappled things—
    For skies of couple-colour as a brinded cow;
       For rose-moles all in stipple upon trout that swim;
Fresh-firecoal chestnut-falls; finches' wings;
    Landscape plotted and pieced—fold, fallow, and plough;
      And áll trades, their gear and tackle and trim.

All things counter, original, spáre, strange;
    Whatever is fickle, frecklèd (who knows how?)
      With swíft, slów; sweet, sóur; adázzle, dím;
He fathers-forth whose beauty is pást change:
                Práise hím.

THE CAGED SKYLARK

As a dare-gale skylark scanted in a dull cage,
    Man's mounting spirit in his bone-house, mean house, dwells—
    That bird beyond the remembering hís free fells;
This in drudgery, day-labouring-out life's age.

Though aloft on turf or perch or poor low stage
    Both sing sometímes the sweetest, sweetest spells,
    Yet both droop deadly sómetimes in their cells
Or wring their barriers in bursts of fear or rage.

Not that the sweet-fowl, song-fowl, needs no rest—
Why, hear him, hear him babble and drop down to his nest,
    But his own nest, wild nest, no prison.

Man's spirit will be flesh-bound, when found at best,
But úncúmberèd: meadow-dówn is nót distréssed
  For a ráinbow fóoting it nor hé for his bónes rísen.

Hurrahing in Harvest

Summer ends now; now, barbrous in beauty, the stooks rise
Around; up above, what wind-walks! what lovely behaviour
Of silk-sack clouds! has wilder, wilful-wavier
Meal-drift moulded ever and melted across skies?

I wálk, I líft up, Í lift úp heart, éyes,
Down all that glory in the heavens to glean our Saviour;
And, éyes, héart, what looks, what lips yet gáve you a
Rapturous love's greeting of realer, of rounder replies?

And the azurous hung hills are his world-wielding shoulder
Majestic—as a stallion stalwart, very-violet-sweet!—
These things, these things were here and but the beholder
Wánting; whích two whén they ónce méet,
The heart rears wings bold and bolder
And hurls for him, O half hurls earth for him off under his feet.

The Lantern out of Doors

Sometimes a lantern moves along the night.
  That interests our eyes. And who gets there?
  I think; where from and bound, I wonder, where,
With, all down darkness wide, his wading light?

Men go by me, whom either beauty bright
    In mould or mind or what not else makes rare:
    They rain against our much-thick and marsh air
Rich beams, till death or distance buys them quite.

Death or distance soon consumes them: wind,
    What most I may eye after, be in at the end
I cannot, and out of sight is out of mind.

Christ minds: Christ's interest, what to avow or amend
    There, éyes them, heart wánts, care háunts, foot fóllows kínd,
Their ránsom, théir rescue, ánd first, fást, last fríend.

The Loss of the Eurydice
foundered March 24, 1878

The Eurydice—it concerned thee, O Lord:
Three hundred souls, O alas! on board,
    Some asleep unawakened, all un-
Warned, eleven fathoms fallen

Where she foundered! One stroke
Felled and furled them, the hearts of oak!
    And flockbells off the aerial
Downs' forefalls beat to the burial.

For did she pride her, freighted fully, on
Bounden bales or a hoard of bullion?—
    Precious passing measure,
Lads and men her lade and treasure.

She had come from a cruise, training seamen—
Men, boldboys soon to be men:
    Must it, worst weather,
Blast bole and bloom together?

No Atlantic squall overwrought her
Or rearing billow of the Biscay water:
    Home was hard at hand
And the blow bore from land.

And you were a liar, O blue March day.
Bright sun lanced fire in the heavenly bay;
    But what black Boreas wrecked her? he
Came equipped, deadly-electric,

A beetling baldbright cloud thorough England
Riding: there did storms not mingle? and
    Hailropes hustle and grind their
Heavengravel? wolfsnow, worlds of it, wind there?

Now Carisbrook keep goes under in gloom;
Now it overvaults Appledurcombe;
    Now near by Ventnor town
It hurls, hurls off Boniface Down.

Too proud, too proud, what a press she bore!
Royal, and all her royals wore.
    Sharp with her, shorten sail!
Too late; lost; gone with the gale.

This was that fell capsize.
As half she had righted and hoped to rise

Death teeming in by her portholes
Raced down decks, round messes of mortals.

Then a lurch forward, frigate and men;
"All hands for themselves" the cry ran then;
    But she who had housed them thither
    Was around them, bound them or wound them with her.

Marcus Hare, high her captain,
Kept to her—care-crowned and wrapped in
    Cheer's death, would follow
His charge through the champ-white water-in-a-wallow,

All under Channel to bury in a beach her
Cheeks: Right, rude of feature,
    He thought he heard say
"Her commander! and thou too, and thou this way."

It is even seen, time's something server,
In mankind's medley a duty-swerver,
    At downright "No or Yes?"
Doffs all, drives full for righteousness.

Sydney Fletcher, Bristol-bred,
(Low lie his mates now on watery bed)
    Takes to the seas and snows
As sheer down the ship goes.

Now her afterdraught gullies him too down;
Now he wrings for breath with the deathgush brown;
    Till a lifebelt and God's will
Lend him a lift from the sea-swill.

Now he shoots short up to the round air;
Now he gasps, now he gazes everywhere;
    But his eyes no cliff, no coast or
Mark makes in the rivelling snowstorm.

Him, after an hour of wintry waves,
A schooner sights, with another, and saves,
    And he boards her in Oh! such joy
He has lost count what came next, poor boy.—

They say who saw one sea-corpse cold
He was all of lovely manly mould,
    Every inch a tar,
Of the best we boast our sailors are.

Look, foot to forelock, how all things suit! he
Is strung by duty, is strained to beauty,
    And brown-as-dawning-skinned
With brine and shine and whirling wind.

O his nimble finger, his gnarled grip!
Leagues, leagues of seamanship
    Slumber in these forsaken
Bones, this sinew, and will not waken.

He was but one like thousands more.
Day and night I deplore
    My people and born own nation,
Fast foundering own generation.

I might let bygones be—our curse
Of ruinous shrine no hand or, worse,

Robbery's hand is busy to
Dress, hoar-hallowèd shrines unvisited;

Only the breathing temple and fleet
Life, this wildworth blown so sweet,
      These daredeaths, ay this crew, in
Unchrist, all rolled in ruin—

Deeply surely I need to deplore it,
Wondering why my master bore it,
      The riving off that race
So at home, time was, to his truth and grace

That a starlight-wender of ours would say
The marvellous Milk was Walsingham Way
      And one—but let be, let be:
More, more than was will yet be.—

O well wept, mother have lost son;
Wept, wife; wept, sweetheart would be one:
      Though grief yield them no good
Yet shed what tears and truelove should.

But to Christ lord of thunder
Crouch; lay knee by earth low under:
      "Holiest, loveliest, bravest,
Save my hero, O Hero savest.

And the prayer thou hearst me making
Have, at the awful overtaking,
      Heard; have heard and granted
Grace that day grace was wanted."

Not that hell knows redeeming,
But for souls sunk in seeming
    Fresh, till doomfire burn all,
Prayer shall fetch pity eternal.

DUNS SCOTUS'S OXFORD

Towery city and branchy between towers;
Cuckoo-echoing, bell-swarmèd, lark-charmèd, rook-racked,
   river-rounded;
The dapple-eared lily below thee; that country and town did
Once encounter in, here coped and poisèd powers;

Thou hast a base and brickish skirt there, sours
That neighbour-nature thy grey beauty is grounded
Best in; graceless growth, thou hast confounded
Rural rural keeping—folk, flocks, and flowers.

Yet ah! this air I gather and I release
He lived on; these weeds and waters, these walls are what
He haunted who of all men most sways my spirits to peace;

Of realty the rarest-veinèd unraveller; a not
Rivalled insight, be rival Italy or Greece;
Who fíred Fránce for Máry withóut spót.

HENRY PURCELL

The poet wishes well to the divine genius of Purcell and praises him that,
whereas other musicians have given utterance to the moods of man's mind,

> he has, beyond that, uttered in notes the very make and species of man as
> created both in him and in all men generally

Have fáir fállen, O fáir, fáir have fállen, so déar
To me, so arch-especial a spirit as heaves in Henry Purcell,
An age is now since passed, since parted; with the reversal
Of the outward sentence low lays him, listed to a heresy, here.

Not mood in him nor meaning, proud fire or sacred fear,
Or love, or pity, or all that sweet notes not his might nursle:
It is the forgèd feature finds me; it is the rehearsal
Of own, of abrupt self there so thrusts on, so throngs the ear.

Let him oh! with his air of angels then lift me, lay me! only I'll
Have an eye to the sakes of him, quaint moonmarks, to his pelted
    plumage under
Wings: so some great stormfowl, whenever he has walked his while

The thunder-purple seabeach, plumèd purple-of-thunder,
If a wuthering of his palmy snow-pinions scatter a colossal smile
Off him, but meaning motion fans fresh our wits with wonder.

THE BUGLER'S FIRST COMMUNION

A bugler boy from barrack (it is over the hill
There)—boy bugler, born, he tells me, of Irish
        Mother to an English sire (he
Shares their best gifts surely, fall how things will),

This very very day came down to us after a boon he on
My late being there begged of me, overflowing

Boon in my bestowing,
Came, I say, this day to it—to a First Communion.

Here he knelt then in regimental red.
Forth Christ from cupboard fetched, how fain I of feet
To his youngster take his treat!
Low-latched in leaf-light housel his too huge godhead.

There! and your sweetest sendings, ah divine,
By it, heavens, befall him! as a heart Christ's darling, dauntless;
Tongue true, vaunt- and tauntless;
Breathing bloom of a chastity in mansex fine.

Frowning and forefending angel-warder
Squander the hell-rook ranks sally to molest him;
March, kind comrade, abreast him;
Dress his days to a dexterous and starlight order.

How it does my heart good, visiting at that bleak hill,
When limber liquid youth, that to all I teach
Yields ténder as a púshed péach,
Hies headstrong to its wellbeing of a self-wise self-will!

Then though Í should tréad túfts of consolation
Dáys áfter, só I in a sort deserve to
And do serve God to serve to
Just such slips of soldiery Christ's royal ration.

Nothing else is like it, no, not all so strains
Us—freshyouth fretted in a bloomfall all portending
That sweet's sweeter ending;
Realm both Christ is heir to and there reigns.

O now well work that sealing sacred ointment!
O for now charms, arms, what bans off bad
      And locks love ever in a lad!
Let mé though sée no more of him, and not disappointment

Those sweet hopes quell whose least me quickenings lift,
In scarlet or somewhere of some day seeing
      That brow and bead of being,
An our day's God's own Galahad. Thóugh this child's drift

Seems bý a divíne doom chánnelled, nor do I cry
Disaster there; but may he not rankle and roam
      In backwheels, though bound home?—
That left to the Lord of the Eucharist, I here lie by;

Recorded only, I have put my lips on pleas
Would brandle adamantine heaven with ride and jar, did
      Prayer go disregarded:
Forward-like, but however, and like favourable heaven heard these.

BINSEY POPLARS
felled 1879

My aspens dear, whose airy cages quelled,
Quelled or quenched in leaves the leaping sun,
Áll félled, félled, are áll félled;
    Of a fresh, and following folded rank
        Not spared, not one
        That dandled a sandalled
    Shadow that swam or sank
On meadow and river and wind-wandering weed-winding bank.

O if we but knew what we do
     When we delve or hew—
   Hack and rack the growing green!
      Since country is so tender
To tóuch, her béing só slénder,
       That, like this sleek and seeing ball
       But a prick will make no eye at all,
     Where we, even where we mean
           To mend her we end her,
      When we hew or delve:
After-comers cannot guess the beauty been.
   Ten or twelve, only ten or twelve
     Strokes of havoc unselve
       The sweet especial scene,
    Rural scene, a rural scene,
    Sweet especial rural scene.

FELIX RANDAL

Félix Rándal the fárrier, O is he déad then? my dúty all énded,
Who have watched his mould of man, big-boned and hardy-
            handsome
Pining, pining, till time when reason rambled in it and some
Fatal four disorders, fleshed there, all contended?

Sickness broke him. Impatient, he cursed at first, but mended
Being anointed and all; though a heavenlier heart began some
Mónths éarlier, since Í had our swéet repriéve and ránsom
Téndered to him. Áh well, God rést him áll road éver he offénded!

This séeing the síck endéars them tó us, us tóo it endéars.
My tongue had taught thee comfort, touch had quenched thy tears,
Thy tears that touched my heart, child, Felix, poor Felix Randal;

How far from them forethought of, all thy more boisterous years,
When thou at the random grim forge, powerful amidst peers,
Didst fettle for the great grey drayhorse his bright and battering
sandal!

SPRING AND FALL:
to a Young Child

Margaret, are you grieving
Over Goldengrove unleaving?
Leaves, like the things of man, you
With your fresh thoughts care for, can you?
Ah! as the heart grows older
It will come to such sights colder
By and by, nor spare a sigh
Though worlds of wanwood leafmeal lie;
And yet you *will* weep and know why.
Now no matter, child, the name:
Sorrow's springs are the same.
Nor mouth had, no nor mind, expressed
What héart héard of, ghóst guéssed:
It is the blight man was born for,
It is Margaret you mourn for.

THE LEADEN ECHO AND THE GOLDEN ECHO
(Maidens' song from St. Winefred's Well)

The Leaden Echo—

How to keep—is there ány any, is there none such, nowhere known
    some, bow or brooch or braid or brace, lace, latch or catch or key to
    keep
Back beauty, keep it, beauty, beauty, beauty, . . . from vanishing away?
Ó is there no frowning of these wrinkles, rankèd wrinkles deep,
Down? no waving off of these most mournful messengers, still
    messengers, sad and stealing messengers of grey?—
No there's none, there's none, O no there's none,
Nor can you long be, what you now are, called fair,
Do what you may do, what, do what you may,
And wisdom is early to despair:
Be beginning; since, no, nothing can be done
To keep at bay
Age and age's evils, hoar hair,
Ruck and wrinkle, drooping, dying, death's worst, winding sheets,
    tombs and worms and tumbling to decay;
So be beginning, be beginning to despair.
O there's none; no no no there's none:
Be beginning to despair, to despair,
Despair, despair, despair, despair.

The Golden Echo—   Spare!
There is one, yes I have one (Hush there!);
Only not within seeing of the sun.
Not within the singeing of the strong sun,
Tall sun's tingeing, or treacherous the tainting of the earth's air,
Somewhere elsewhere there is (ah well where!) one,

One. Yes I can tell such a key, I do know such a place,
Where whatever's prizèd and passes of us, everything that's fresh and
    fast flying of us, seems to us sweet of us and swiftly away with, done
    away with, undone,
Undone, done with, soon done with, and yet dearly and dangerously
    sweet
Of us, the wimpledwater-dimpled, not-by-morning-matchèd face,
The flower of beauty, fleece of beauty, too too apt to, ah! to fleet,
Never fleets more, fastened with the tenderest truth
To its own best being and its loveliness of youth: it is an everlastingness
    of, O it is an all youth!
Cóme then, your ways and airs and looks, locks, maidengear, gallantry
    and gaiety and grace,
Winning ways, airs innocent, maidenmanners, sweet looks, loose
    locks, long locks, lovelocks, gaygear, going gallant, girlgrace—
Resign them, sign them, seal them, send them, motion them with
    breath,
And with sighs soaring, soaring sighs, deliver
Them; beauty-in-the-ghost, deliver it, early now, long before death
Give beauty back, beauty, beauty, beauty, back to God,
    beauty's self and beauty's giver.
See; not a hair is, not an eyelash, not the least lash lost; every hair
Is, hair of the head, numbéred.
Nay, what we had lighthanded left in surly the mere mould
Will have waked and have waxed and have walked with the wind
    what while we slept,
This side, that side hurling a heavy-headed hundredfold
What while we, while we slumbered.
O then, weary then whý should we tread? O why are we so haggard
    at the heart, so care-coiled, care-killed, so fagged, so fashed, so
    cogged, so cumbered,
When the thing we freely fórfeit is kept with fonder a care,

Fonder a care kept than we could have kept it, kept
Far with fonder a care (and we, we should have lost it) finer, fonder
A care kept.—Where kept? do but tell us where kept, where.—
Yonder.—What high as that! We follow, now we follow.—Yonder,
   yes yonder, yonder,
Yonder.

RIBBLESDALE

Earth, sweet Earth, sweet landscape, with leavès throng
And louchèd low grass, heaven that dost appeal
To with no tongue to plead, no heart to feel;
That canst but only be, but dost that long—

Thou canst but be, but that thou well dost; strong
Thy plea with him who dealt, nay does now deal,
Thy lovely dale down thus and thus bids reel
Thy river, and o'er gives all to rack or wrong.

And what is Earth's eye, tongue, or heart else, where
Else, but in dear and dogged man? Ah, the heir
To his own selfbent so bound, so tied to his turn,

To thriftless reave both our rich round world bare
And none reck of world after, this bids wear
Earth brows of such care, care and dear concern.

The Blessed Virgin compared
to the Air we Breathe

Wild air, world-mothering air,
Nestling me everywhere,
That each eyelash or hair
Girdles; goes home betwixt
the fleeciest, frailest-flixed
Snowflake; that's fairly mixed
With, riddles, and is rife
In every least thing's life;
This needful, never spent,
And nursing element;
My more than meat and drink,
My meal at every wink;
This air, which, by life's law,
My lung must draw and draw
Now but to breathe its praise,
Minds me in many ways
Of her who nót only
Gave God's infinity
Dwindled to infancy
Welcome in womb and breast,
Birth, milk, and all the rest
But mothers each new grace
That does now reach our race—
Mary Immaculate,
Merely a woman, yet
Whose presence, power is
Great as no goddess's
Was deemèd, dreamèd; who
This one work has to do—

Let all God's glory through,
God's glory which would go
Through her and from her flow
Off, and no way but so.
    I say that we are wound
With mercy round and round
As if with air: the same
Is Mary, more by name.
She, wild web, wondrous robe,
Mantles the guilty globe,
Since God has let dispense
Her prayers his providence:
Nay, more than almoner,
The sweet alms' self is her
And men are meant to share
Her life as life does air.
    If I have understood,
She holds high motherhood
Towards all our ghostly good
And plays in grace her part
About man's beating heart,
Laying, like air's fine flood,
The deathdance in his blood;
Yet no part but what will
Be Christ our Saviour still.
Of her flesh he took flesh:
He does take fresh and fresh,
Though much the mystery how,
Not flesh but spirit now
And makes, O marvellous!
New Nazareths in us,

Where she shall yet conceive
Him, morning, noon, and eve;
New Bethlems, and he born
There, evening, noon, and morn—
Bethlem or Nazareth,
Men here may draw like breath
More Christ and baffle death;
Who, born so, comes to be
New self and nobler me
In each one and each one
More makes, when all is done,
Both God's and Mary's Son.

    Again, look overhead
How air is azurèd;
O how! Nay do but stand
Where you can lift your hand
Skywards: rich, rich it laps
Round the four fingergaps.
Yet such a sapphire-shot,
Charged, steepèd sky will not
Stain light. Yes, mark you this:
It does no prejudice.
The glass-blue days are those
When every colour glows,
Each shape and shadow shows.
Blue be it: this blue heaven
The seven or seven times seven
Hued sunbeam will transmit
Perfect, not alter it.
Or if there does some soft,
On things aloof, aloft,

Bloom breathe, that one breath more
Earth is the fairer for.
Whereas did air not make
This bath of blue and slake
His fire, the sun would shake,
A blear and blinding ball
With blackness bound, and all
The thick stars round him roll
Flashing like flecks of coal,
Quartz-fret, or sparks of salt,
In grimy vasty vault.

    So God was God of old:
A mother came to mould
Those limbs like ours which are
What must make our daystar
Much dearer to mankind;
Whose glory bare would blind
Or less would win man's mind.
Through her we may see him
Made sweeter, not made dim,
And her hand leaves his light
Sifted to suit our sight.

    Be thou then, O thou dear
Mother, my atmosphere;
My happier world, wherein
To wend and meet no sin;
Above me, round me lie
Fronting my forward eye
With sweet and scarless sky;
Stir in my ears, speak there
Of God's love, O live air,

Of patience, penance, prayer:
World-mothering air, air wild,
Wound with thee, in thee isled,
Fold home, fast fold thy child.

"I WAKE AND FEEL"

I wake and feel the fell of dark, not day.
What hours, O what black hours we have spent
This night! what sights you, heart, saw, ways you went!
And more must, in yet longer light's delay.

With witness I speak this. But where I say
Hours I mean years, mean life. And my lament
Is cries countless, cries like dead letters sent
To dearest him that lives alas! away.

I am gall, I am heartburn. God's most deep decree
Bitter would have me taste: my taste was me;
Bones built in me, flesh filled, blood brimmed the curse.

Selfyeast of spirit a dull dough sours. I see
The lost are like this, and their scourge to be
As I am mine, their sweating selves; but worse.

"NO WORST"

No worst, there is none. Pitched past pitch of grief,
More pangs will, schooled at forepangs, wilder wring.

Comforter, where, where is your comforting?
Mary, mother of us, where is your relief?
My cries heave, herds-long; huddle in a main, a chief-
Woe, wórld-sorrow; on an áge-old ánvil wínce and síng—
Then lull, then leave off. Fury had shrieked "No ling-
Ering! Let me be fell: force I must be brief."
O the mind, mind has mountains; cliffs of fall
Frightful, sheer, no-man-fathomed. Hold them cheap
May who ne'er hung there. Nor does long our small
Durance deal with that steep or deep. Here! creep,
Wretch, under a comfort serves in a whirlwind: all
Life death does end and each day dies with sleep.

To what serves Mortal Beauty?

To what serves mortal beauty— | dangerous; does set danc-
Ing blood—the O-seal-that-so | feature, flung prouder form
Than Purcell tune lets tread to? | See: it does this: keeps warm
Men's wit to the things that are; | to what good means—where a glance
Master more may than gaze, | gaze out of countenance.
Those lovely lads once, wet-fresh | windfalls of war's storm,
How then should Gregory, a father, | have gleanèd else from swarm-
Èd Rome? But God to a nation | deal that day's dear chance.
To man, that once would worship | block or barren stone,
Our law says: love what are | love's worthiest, were all known;
World's loveliest—men's selves. Self | flashes off frame and face.
What do then? how meet beauty? | Merely meet it; own,
Home at heart, heaven's sweet gift; | then leave, let that alone.
Yea, wish that though, wish all, | God's better beauty, grace.

(Carrion Comfort)

Not, I'll not, carrion comfort, Despair, not feast on thee;
Not untwist—slack they may be—these last strands of man
In me ór, most weary, cry *I can no more*. I can;
Can something, hope, wish day come, not choose not to be.

But ah, but O thou terrible, why wouldst thou rude on me
Thy wring-earth right foot rock? lay a lionlimb against me? scan
With darksome devouring eyes my bruisèd bones? and fan,
O in turns of tempest, me heaped there; me frantic to avoid thee and
    flee?

Why? That my chaff might fly; my grain lie, sheer and clear.
Nay in all that toil, that coil, since (seems) I kissed the rod,
Hand rather, my heart lo! lapped strength, stole joy, would laugh,
    cheer.

Cheer whóm though? The héro whose héaven-handling flúng me,
    fóot tród
Me? or mé that fóught him? O whích one? is it eách one? That
    níght, that year
Of now done darkness I wretch lay wrestling with (my God!) my God.

(The Soldier)

Yes. Whý do we áll, seeing of a | soldier, bless him? bléss
Our redcoats, our tars? Both | thése being, the greater part,
But frail clay, nay but foul clay. | Hére it is: the heart,
Since, proud, it calls the calling | manly, gives a guess

That, hopes that, mákesbelieve, | the men must be no less;
It fancies, feigns, deems, déars | the artist after his art;
And fain will find as sterling | all as all is smart
And scarlet wéar the spirit of war thére express.
Mark Christ our King. He knows war, served this soldiering through;
He of all can reave a rope best. | Thee he bides in bliss
Now, and seeing somewhere some man | do all that man can do,
For love he léans forth, needs | his neck must fall on, kiss,
And cry "O Christ-done deed! | So God-made-flesh does too:
Were I come o'er again" cries | Christ "it should be this."

"THEE, GOD, I COME FROM"

Thee, God, I come from, to thee go,
All dáy long I like fountain flow
From thy hand out, swayed about
Mote-like in thy mighty glow.

What I know of thee I bless,
As acknowledging thy stress
On my being and as seeing
Something of thy holiness.

Once I turned from thee and hid,
Bound on what thou hadst forbid;
Sow the wind I would; I sinned:
I repent of what I did.

Bad I am, but yet thy child.
Father, be thou reconciled.

Spare thou me, since I see
With thy might that thou art mild.

I have life left with me still
And thy purpose to fulfill;
Yea a debt to pay thee yet:
Help me, sir, and so I will.

But thou bidst, and just thou art,
Me shew mercy from my heart
Towards my brother, every other
Man my mate and counterpart.

   .   .   .   .   .

Jesus Christ sacrificed
On the cross

Moulded, he, in maiden's womb,
Lived and died and from the tomb
Rose in power and is our
Judge that comes to deal our doom.

"MY OWN HEART"

My own heart let me more have pity on; let
Me live to my sad self hereafter kind,
Charitable; not live this tormented mind
With this tormented mind tormenting yet.

I cast for comfort I can no more get
By groping round my comfortless than blind

Eyes in their dark can day or thirst can find
Thirst's all-in-all a world of wet.

Soul, self; come, poor Jackself, I do advise
You, jaded, lét be; call off thoughts awhile
Elsewhere; leave comfort root-room; let joy size

At God knows when to God knows what; whose smile
'S not wrung, see you; unforeseentimes rather—as skies
Betweenpie mountains—lights a lovely mile.

SPELT FROM SIBYL'S LEAVES

Earnest, earthless, equal, attuneable, | vaulty, voluminous, . . .
    stupendous
Evening strains to be tíme's vást, | womb-of-all, home-of-all, hearse-of-
    all night.
Her fond yellow hornlight wound to the west, | her wild hollow
    hoarlight hung to the height
Waste; her earliest stars, earlstars, | stars principal, overbend us,
Fíre-féaturing héaven. For éarth | her béing has unbóund; her dápple
    is at énd, as-
Tray or aswarm, all throughther, in throngs; | self ín self stéepèd and
    páshed—qúite
Disremembering, dismembering | all now. Heart, you round me right
With: Óur évening is óver us; óur night | whélms, whélms, ánd will
    énd us.
Only the beakleaved boughs dragonish | damask the tool-smooth bleak
    light; black,

Ever so black on it. Óur tale, O óur oracle! | Lét life, wáned, ah lét life
     wínd
Off hér once skéined stained véined varíety | upon, áll on twó spools;
     párt, pen, páck
Now her áll in twó flocks, twó folds—bláck, white; | ríght, wrong;
     réckon but, réck but, mínd
But thése two; wáre of a wórld where bút these | twó tell, éach off the
     óther; of a ráck
Where, selfwrung, selfstrung, sheathe- and shelterless, | thoúghts
     agáinst thoughts ín groans grínd.

HARRY PLOUGHMAN

Hard as hurdle arms, with a broth of goldish flue
Breathed round; the rack of ribs; the scooped flank; lank
Rope-over thigh; knee-nave; and barrelled shank—
     Head and foot, shouldér and shank—
By a grey eye's heed steered well, one crew, fall to;
Stand at stress. Each limb's barrowy brawn, his thew
That onewhere curded, onewhere sucked or sank—
     Soared ór sank—,
Though as a beechbole firm, finds his, as at a rollcall, rank
And features, in flesh, what deed he each must do—
     His sinew-service where do.
He leans to it, Harry bends, look. Back, elbow, and liquid waist
In him, all quáil to the wallowing o' the plough. 'S cheek crímsons;
     curls
Wag or crossbridle, in a wind lifted, windlaced—
     Wind-lilylocks-laced;

Churlsgrace too, chíld of Amansstrength, how it hángs or hurls
Them—broad in bluff hide his frowning feet lashed! raced
With, along them, cragiron under and cold furls—
      With-a-fountain's shining-shot furls.

That Nature is a Heraclitean Fire and of the comfort of the Resurrection

Cloud-puffball, torn tufts, tossed pillows | flaunt forth, then chevy
      on an air—
Built thoroughfare: heaven-roysterers, in gay-gangs | they throng;
      they glitter in marches.
Down roughcast, down dazzling whitewash, | whenever an elm
      arches,
Shivelights and shadowtackle in long | lashes lace, lance, and pair.
Delightfully the bright wind boisterous | ropes, wrestles, beats earth
      bare
Of yestertempest's creases; in pool and rutpeel parches
Squandering ooze to squeezed | dough, crust, dust; stanches, starches
Squadroned masks and manmarks | treadmire toil there
Footfretted in it. Million-fuelèd, | nature's bonfire burns on.
But quench her bonniest, dearest | to her, her clearest-selvèd
      spark
Man, how fast his firedint, | his mark on mind, is gone!
Both are in an únfathomable, all is in an enormous dark
Drowned. O pity and indig | nation! Manshape, that shone
Sheer off, disseveral, a star, | death blots black out; nor mark
      Is any of him at all so stark
But vastness blurs and time | beats level. Enough! the Resurrection,
A heart's-clarion! Away grief's gasping, | joyless days, dejection.
      Across my foundering deck shone

A beacon, an eternal beam. | Flesh fade, and mortal trash
Fall to the residuary worm; | world's wildfire, leave but ash:
                    In a flash, at a trumpet crash,
I am all at once what Christ is, | since he was what I am, and
This Jack, joke, poor potsherd, | patch, matchwood, immortal
        diamond,
                    Is immortal diamond.

IN HONOUR OF
ST. ALPHONSUS RODRIGUEZ
Laybrother of the Society of Jesus upon the
first falling of his feast after his canonisation
For the College of Palms in the Island
of Majorca, where the saint lived for 40 years as
Hall porter

Glory is a flame off exploit, so we say,
And those fell strokes that once scarred flesh, scored shield,
Should tongue that time now, trumpet now that field,
Record, and on the fighter forge the day.
On Christ they do, they on the martyr may;
But where war is within, what sword we wield
Not seen, the heroic breast not outward-steeled,
Earth hears no hurtle then from fiercest fray.
Yet, he that hews out mountain, continent,
Earth, all, at last; who, with fine increment
Trickling, veins violets and tall trees makes more
Could crowd career with conquest while there went
Those years and years by of world without event
That in Majorca Alfonso watched the door.

JUSTUS QUIDEM TU ES, DOMINE,

si disputem tecum; verumtamen justa loquar ad te: quare via impiorum
prosperatur? etc[6]
(JER. 12:1)

Thou art indeed just, Lord, if I contend
With thee; but, sir, so what I plead is just.
Why do sinners' ways prosper? and why must
Disappointment all I endeavour end?

Wert thou my enemy, O thou my friend,
How wouldst thou worse, I wonder, than thou dost
Defeat, thwart me? Oh, the sots and thralls of lust
Do in spare hours more thrive than I that spend,

Sir, life upon thy cause. See, banks and brakes
Now, leavèd how thick! lacèd they are again
With fretty chervil, look, and fresh wind shakes

Them; birds build—but not I build; no, but strain,
Time's eunuch, and not breed one work that wakes.
Mine, O thou lord of life, send my roots rain.

---

[6]"Righteous art Thou, O Lord, when I complain to Thee; yet I would plead my case
before Thee. Why does the way of the wicked prosper?" (RSV)

Early Diaries

Flick, fillip, flip, fleck, flake.

Flick means to touch or strike lightly as with the end of a whip, a finger etc. To *fleck* is the next tone above flick, still meaning to touch or strike lightly (and leave a mark of the touch or stroke) but in a broader less slight manner. Hence substantively a *fleck* is a piece of light, colour, substance etc. looking as though shaped or produced by such touches. *Flake* is a broad and decided *fleck,* a thin plate of something, the tone above it. Their connection is more clearly seen in the applications of the words to natural objects than in explanations. It would seem that *fillip* generally pronounced *flip* is a variation of *flick,* which however seems connected with *fly, flee, flit,* meaning to make fly off. Key to meaning of *flick, fleck* and *flake* is that of striking or cutting off the surface of a thing; in *flick* (as to flick off a fly) something little or light from the surface, while *flake* is a thin scale of surface. *Flay* is therefore connected, perhaps *flitch.*

January 23, 1866

For Lent. No pudding on Sundays. No tea except if to keep me awake and then without sugar. Meat only once a day. No verses in Passion Week or on Fridays. No lunch or meat on Fridays. Not to sit in armchair except can work in no other way. Ash Wednesday and Good Friday bread and water.

Journal

[1866]

July 17. Dull, curds-and-whey clouds faintly at times.—It was this night I believe but possibly the next that I saw clearly the impossibility of staying in the Church of England, but resolved to say nothing to anyone till three months are over, that is the end of the Long, and then of course to take no step till after my Degree.

[1867]

Aug. 22. Bright.—Walked to Finchley and turned down a lane to a field where I sketched an appletree. Their sprays against the sky are gracefully curved and the leaves looping over edge them, as it looks, with rows of scales. In something the same way I saw some tall young slender wych-elms of thin growth the leaves of which enclosed the light in successive eyebrows. From the spot where I sketched—under an oak, beyond a brook, and reached by the above green lane between a park-ground and a pretty field—there was a charming view, the field, lying then on the right of the lane, being a close-shaven smoothly-rounded shield of bright green ended near the high road by a row of viol-headed or flask-shaped elms—not rounded merely but squared—of much beauty—dense leafing, rich dark colour, ribs and spandrils of timber garlanded with leaf between tree and tree. But what most struck me was a pair of ashes in going up the lane again. The further one was the finer—a globe-ish just-sided head with one launching-out member on the right; the nearer one was more naked and horny. By taking a few steps one could pass the further behind the nearer or make the stems close, either coincidingly, so far as disagreeing outlines will coincide, or allowing a slit on either side, or again on either side making a broader stem than either would make alone. It was this which was so beautiful—making a noble shaft and base to the double tree, which was crested by the horns of the nearer ash and shaped on the right by the bosom of the hinder one with its springing bough. The outline of the double stem was beautiful to whichever of the two sides you slid the hinder tree—in one (not, I think, in both) shaft-like and narrowing at the ground. Besides I saw how great the richness and subtlety is of the curves in the clusters, both in the forward bow mentioned before and in some most graceful hangers on the other side: it combines somewhat-slanted outward strokes with rounding, but I cannot very well characterise it now.—Elm-leaves:—they shine much in the sun—bright green when near from underneath but higher up they look olive: their shapelessness in the flat is from their being made, διὰ το πεφυχέναι [through growth], to be dimpled and dog's-eared: their leaf-growth is in this point more rudimentary than that of oak, ash, beech, etc that the leaves lie in long rows and do not subdivide or have central knots but tooth or cog their woody twigs.

[1868]
[Holiday in Switzerland]

July 11. Fine.

We took a guide up the Wylerhorn but the top being clouded dismissed him and stayed up the mountain, lunching by a waterfall. Presently after long climbing—for there was a good chance of a clearance—we nearly reached the top, when a cloud coming on thick frightened me back: had we gone on we should have had the view, for it cleared quite. Still we saw the neighbouring mountains well. The snow is often cross-harrowed and lies too in the straightest paths as though artificial, which again comes from the planing. In the sheet it glistens yellow to the sun. How fond of and warped to the mountains it would be easy to become! For every cliff and limb and edge and jutty has its own nobility.—Two boys came down the mountain yodelling.—We saw the snow in the hollows for the first time. In one the surface was crisped across the direction of the cleft and the other way, that is across the broader crisping and down the stream, combed: the stream ran below and smoke came from the hollow: the edge of the snow hewn in curves as if by moulding-planes.—Crowd of mountain flowers—gentians; gentianellas; blood-red lucerne; a deep blue glossy spiked flower like plantain, flowering gradually up the spike, so that at the top it looks like clover or honeysuckle; rich big harebells glistening black like the cases of our veins when dry and heated from without; and others. All the herbage enthronged with every fingered or fretted leaf.— Firs very tall, with the swell of the branching on the outer side of the slope so that the peaks seem to point inwards to the mountain peak, like the lines of the Parthenon, and the outline melodious and moving on many focuses.—I wore my pagharee and turned it with harebells below and gentians in two rows above like double pan-pipes.—In coming down we lost our way and each had a dangerous slide down the long wet grass of a steep slope.

Waterfalls not only skeined but silky too—one saw it from the inn across the meadows: at one quain of the rock the water glistened above and took shadow below, and the rock was reddened a little way each side with the wet, which sets off the silkiness.

Goat-flocks, each goat with its bell.

Ashes here are often pollarded and look different from ours and they give off their sprays at the outline in marked parallels justifying the Italian painters.

July 15. Showers; little sun.

Walked to the Hôtel Bellevue on the Little Scheidegg.

The mountains and in particular the Silberhorn are shaped and nippled like the sand in an hourglass and the Silberhorn has a sub-sidiary pyramidal peak napped sharply down the sides. Then one of their beauties is in nearly vertical places the fine pleatings of the snow running to or from one another, like the newness of lawn in an alb and sometimes cut off short as crisp as celery.

There are round one of the heights of the Jungfrau two ends or falls of a glacier. If you took the skin of a white tiger or the deep fell of some other animal and swung it tossing high in the air and then cast it out before you it would fall and so clasp and lap round anything in its way just as this glacier does and the fleece would part in the same rifts: you must suppose a lazuli under-flix to appear. The spraying out of one end I tried to catch but it would have taken hours: it was this which first made me think of a tiger-skin, and it ends in tongues and points like the tail and claws: indeed the ends of the glaciers are knotted or knuckled like talons. Above, in a plane nearly parallel to the eye, becoming thus foreshortened, it forms saddle-curves with dips and swells.

The view was not good: a few times we saw the Silberhorn but the Eiger never clearly and the Jungfrau itself scarcely or not at all.

It is curious how blue the glimpses of the mountain-sides and valleys look through the lifting cloud.

July 18. Up a little after sunrise but rain was falling and nothing worth seeing but the orange slit in the E. Then it became fine; dull afternoon; fine evening.

In coming down the Faulhorn saw the Finster Aarhorn at last, lonely, standing like a high-gabled steeple. The two heights of the Viescherhörner group are striking too, rising like thorns (as many *hörner* are like thorns or talons) from the level ridged wall which forms the theatre of the Grindelwald glacier.

Rushing streams may be described as inscaped ordinarily in pillows—and upturned troughs.

We lunched at the Baths of Rosenlaui and walked on to Meyringen down the valley of the Reichenbach in torrent. Sycomores grew on the slopes of the valley, scantily leaved, sharply quained and accidented by

perhaps the valley winds, and often most gracefully inscaped.—On
the wall of the cliff bounding the valley on the further side of the river
was a bright silver-tackled waterfall parted into slender shanks.

When Meyringen came in sight in the broader thwart valley
below we sat on a little bridge over the Reichenbach there narrowed
in, all leaved over, and rushing from one cornered rocky chamber to
another. I saw that below the cuffs or long lips of lather that form
there descended a webby space of foamy water. On the one side of
the bridge an ash rose with eye-taking sky-clusters, the leaves mak-
ing the outlines of their two sides smartly cross and recross and so
giving the disputed bat's-wing.

Then we saw the three falls of the Reichenbach. The upper one is
the biggest. At the take-off it falls in discharges of rice or meal but each
cluster as it descends sharpens and tapers, and from halfway down the
whole cascade is inscaped in fretted falling vandykes in each of which
the frets or points, just like the startings of a just-lit lucifer match, keep
shooting in races, one beyond the other, to the bottom. The vapour
which beats up from the impact of the falling water makes little feeder
rills down the rocks and these catching and running in drops along the
sharp ledges in the rock are shaken and delayed and chased along
them and even cut off and blown upwards by the blast of the vapour as
it rises: saw the same thing at Handeck too.—In the second fall when
facing the great limbs in which the water is packed saw well how they
are tretted like open sponge or light bread-crumb where the yeast has
supped in the texture in big and little holes.

July 19, 1868. Sunday, but no Catholics, I found, at Meyringen.
The day fine.

Walked up the valley of the Aar, sallow-coloured and torrent, to
the Grimsel. The heights bounding the valley soon became a mingle
of lilac and green, the first the colour of the rock, the other the grass
crestings, and seemed to group above in crops and rounded but-
tresses, yet to be cut sharp in horizontal or leaning planes below.

We came up with a guide who reminded me of F. John. He took E.B.'s knapsack and on finding the reason why I would not let him take mine said "Le bon Dieu n'est pas comme ça." The man probably was a rational Protestant; if a Catholic at least he rationalized gracefully, as they do in Switzerland.

At a turn in the road the foam-cuffs in the river, looked down upon, were of the crispiest endive spraying.

We lunched at Guttannen, where there was that strange party of Americans.

I was arguing about the planing of rocks and made a sketch of two in the Aar, and after that it was strange, for Nature became Nemesis, so precise they were, and E.B. himself pointed out two which looked, he said, as if they had been sawn. And of the hills themselves it could sometimes be seen, but on the other hand the sides of the valley often descended in trending sweeps of vertical section and so met at the bottom.

At times the valley opened in *cirques,* amphitheatres, enclosing levels of plain, and the river then ran between flaky flat-fish isles made of cindery lily-white stones.—In or near one of these openings the guide cries out "Voulez-vous une Alp-rose?" and up he springs the side of the hill and brings us each bunches of flowers down.

In one place over a smooth table of rock came slipping down a blade of water looking like and as evenly crisped as fruitnets let drop and falling slack.

We saw Handeck waterfall. It is in fact the meeting of two waters, the right the Aar sallow and jade-coloured, the left a smaller stream of clear lilac foam. It is the greatest fall we have seen. The lower half is hidden in spray. I watched the great bushes of foam-water, the texture of branchings and water-spandrils which makes them up. At their outsides nearest the rock they gave off showers of drops strung together into little quills which sprang out in fans.

On crossing the Aar again there was as good a fall as some we have paid to see, all in jostling foam-bags.

Across the valley too we saw the fall of the Gelmer—like milk chasing round blocks of coal; or a girdle or long purse of white weighted with irregular black rubies, carelessly thrown aside and lying in jutty bends, with a black clasp of the same stone at the top— for those were the biggest blocks, squared, and built up, as it happened, in lessening stories, and the cascade enclosed them on the right and left hand with its foam; or once more like the skin of a white snake square-pied with black.

July 26. Sunday. There was no church nearer than Valtour-nanches, but there was to be mass said in a little chapel for the guides going up with Tyndal at two o'clock in the morning and so I got up for this, my burnt face in a dreadful state and running. We went down with lanterns. It was an odd scene: two of the guides or porters served; the noise of a torrent outside accompanied the priest. Then to bed again.

Day fine. We did not get a completely clear view of the Matter-horn from this side.

In the afternoon we walked down the valley, which is beautiful, to Valtournanches.—We passed a gorge at the end of which it was curious to see a tree rubbing and ruffling with the water at the neck just above a fall.—Then we saw a grotto, that is deep and partly covered chambers of rock through which the torrent river runs.—A little beyond, I think, was a wayside chapel with a woman kneeling at a window a long time.—Further, across the valley a pretty village, the houses white, deep-eaved, pierced with small square windows at effective distances, and crossed with balconies, and above, a grove of ash or sycamore or both, sprayed all one way like water-weed beds in a running stream, very English-looking.— Beyond again, in midst of a slope of meadow slightly pulled like an unsteady and swelling surface of water, some ashes growing in a beautifully clustered "bouquet," the skeleton as below—the inward bend of the left-hand stem being partly real, partly apparent and helped by τύχη τέχνην στεργούση["by chance that loves art"].—Dim mountains down the valley red in the sunset.

[1870]

March 12—A fine sunset: the higher sky dead clear blue bridged by a broad slant causeway rising from right to left of wisped or grass cloud, the wisps lying across; the sundown yellow, moist with light but ending at the top in a foam of delicate white pearling and spotted with big tufts of cloud in colour russet between brown and purple but edged with brassy light. But what I note it all for is this: before I had always taken the sunset and the sun as quite out of gauge with each other, as indeed physically they are for the eye after looking at the sun is blunted to everything else and if you look at the rest of the sunset you must cover the sun, but today I inscaped them together and made the sun the true eye and ace of the whole, as it is. It was all active and tossing out light and started as strongly forward from the field as a long stone or a boss in the knop of the chalice-stem: it is indeed by stalling it so that it falls into scape with the sky.

May 12—One day when the bluebells were in bloom I wrote the following. I do not think I have ever seen anything more beautiful than the bluebell I have been looking at. I know the beauty of our Lord by it. It[s inscape][7] is [mixed of] strength and grace, like an ash [tree]. The head is strongly drawn over [backwards] and arched down like

[7]Hopkins's own brackets.

a cutwater [drawing itself back from the line of the keel].
The lines of the bells strike and overlie this, rayed but not
symmetrically, some lie parallel. They look steely against
[the] paper, the shades lying between the bells and behind the cock-
led petal-ends and nursing up the precision of their distinctness, the
petal-ends themselves being delicately lit. Then there is the straight-
ness of the trumpets in the bells softened by the slight entasis and
[by] the square splay of the mouth. One bell, the lowest, some way
detached and carried on a longer foot-stalk, touched out with the
tips of the petals an oval / not like the rest in a plane perpendicular to
the axis of the bell but a little atilt, and so with [the] square-in-
rounding turns of the petals. . . . There is a little drawing of this
detached bell.—It looks square-cut in the original

[1871]

The spring weather began with March about

I have been watching clouds this spring and evaporation, for
instance over our Lenten chocolate. It seems as if the heat by *aestus,*
throes / one after another threw films of vapour off as boiling water
throws off steam under films of water, that is bubbles. One query
then is whether these films contain gas or no. The film seems to be
set with tiny bubbles which gives it a grey and grained look. By
throes perhaps which represent the moments at which the evener
stress of the heat has overcome the resistance of the surface or of the
whole liquid. It would be reasonable then to consider the films as the
shell of gas-bubbles and the grain on them as a network of bubbles
condensed by the air as the gas rises.—Candle smoke goes by just the
same laws, the visible film being here of unconsumed substance, not
hollow bubbles. The throes can be perceived / like the thrills of a
candle in the socket: this is precisely to *reech,* whence *reek.* They may

by a breath of air be laid again and then shew like grey wisps on the surface—which shews their part-solidity. They seem to be drawn off the chocolate as you might take up a napkin between your fingers that covered something, not so much from here or there as from the whole surface at once reech, so that the film is perceived at the edges and makes in fact a collar or ring just within the walls all round the cup; it then draws together in a cowl like a candleflame but not regularly or without a break: the question is why. Perhaps in perfect stillness it would not but the air breathing it aside entangles it with itself. The film seems to rise not quite simultaneously but to peel off as if you were tearing cloth; then giving an end forward like the corner of a handkerchief and beginning to coil it makes a long wavy hose you may sometimes look down, as a ribbon or a carpenter's shaving may be made to do. Higher running into frets and silvering in the sun with the endless coiling, the soft bound of the general motion and yet the side lurches sliding into some particular pitch it makes a baffling and charming sight.—Clouds however solid they may look far off are I think wholly made of film in the sheet or in the tuft. The bright woolpacks that pelt before a gale in a clear sky are in the tuft and you can see the wind unravelling and rending them finer than any sponge till within one easy reach overhead they are

 morselled to nothing and consumed—it depends of course on their size. Possibly each tuft in forepitch or in origin is quained and a crystal. Rarer and wilder packs have sometimes film in the sheet, which may be caught as it turns on the edge of the cloud like an outlying eyebrow. The one in which I saw this was in a north-east wind, solid but not crisp, white like the white of egg, and bloated-looking

What you look hard at seems to look hard at you, hence the true and the false instress of nature. One day early in March when long

streamers were rising from over Kemble End one large flake loop-shaped, not a streamer but belonging to the string, moving too slowly to be seen, seemed to cap and fill the zenith with a white shire of cloud. I looked long up at it till the tall height and the beauty of the scaping—regularly curled knots springing if I remember from fine stems, like foliation in wood or stone—had strongly grown on me. It changed beautiful changes, growing more into ribs and one stretch of running into branching like coral. Unless you refresh the mind from time to time you cannot always remember or believe how deep the inscape in things is

March 14—Bright morning, pied skies, hail. In the afternoon the wind was from the N., very cold; long bows of soft grey cloud straining the whole heaven but spanning the skyline with a slow entasis which left a strip of cold porcelain blue. The long ribs or girders were as rollers / across the wind, not in it, but across them there lay fine grass-ends, sided off down the perspective, as if locks of vapour blown free from the main ribs down the wind. Next day and next snow. Then in walking I saw the water-runs in the sand of unusual delicacy and the broken blots of snow in the dead bents of the hedge-banks I could find a square scaping in which helped the eye over another hitherto disordered field of things. (And if you look well at big pack-clouds overhead you will soon find a strong large quaining and squaring in them which makes each pack impressive and whole.) Pendle was beautiful: the face of snow on it and the tracks or gulleys which streaked and parted this well shaped out its roundness and boss and marked the slow tune of its long shoulder. One time it lay above a near hill of green field which, with the lands in it lined and plated by snow, was striped like a zebra: this Pendle repeated finer and dimmer

March 17—In the morning clouds chalky and milk-coloured, with remarkable oyster-shell moulding. (From a rough pencil sketch)

Between eleven and twelve at night a shock of earthquake

End of March and beginning of April—This is the time to study inscape in the spraying of trees, for the swelling buds carry them to a pitch which the eye could not else gather—for out of much much more, out of little not much, out of nothing nothing: in these sprays at all events there is a new world of inscape. The male ashes are very boldly jotted with the heads of the bloom which tuft the outer ends of the branches. The staff of each of these branches is closely knotted with the places where buds are or have been, so that it is something like a finger which has been tied up with string and keeps the marks. They are in knops of a pair, one on each side, and the knops are set alternately, at crosses with the knops above and the knops below, the bud of course is a short smoke-black pointed nail-head or beak pierced of four lids or nippers. Below it, like the hollow below the eye or the piece between the knuckle and the root of the nail, is a half-moon-shaped sill as if once chipped from the wood and this gives the twig its quaining in the outline. When the bud breaks at first it shews a heap of fruity purplish anthers looking something like unripe elder-berries but these push open into richly-branched tree-pieces coloured buff and brown, shaking out loads of pollen, and drawing the tuft as a whole into peaked quains—mainly four, I think, two bigger and two smaller

The bushes in the woods and hedgerows are spanned over and twisted upon by the woody cords of the honeysuckle: the cloves of leaf these bear are some purple, some grave green. But the young green of the briars is gay and neat and smooth as if cut in ivory.—One bay or hollow of Hodder Wood is curled all over with bright green garlic

The sycomores are quite the earliest trees out: some have been fully out some days (April 15). The behaviour of the opening clusters is very beautiful and when fully opened not the single leaves but the whole tuft is strongly templed like the belly of a drum or bell

The half-opened wood-sorrel leaves, the center or spring of the leaflets rising foremost and the leaflets dropping back like ears leaving straight-chipped clefts between them, look like some green lettering and cut as sharp as dice

The white violets are broader and smell; the blue, scentless and finer made, have a sharper whelking and a more winged recoil in the leaves

Take a *few* primroses in a glass and the instress of—brilliancy, sort of starriness: I have not the right word—so simple a flower gives is remarkable. It is, I think, due to the strong swell given by the deeper yellow middle

"The young lambs bound As to the tabour's sound."

They toss and toss: it is as if it were the earth that flung them, not themselves. It is the pitch of graceful agility when we think that.— April 16—Sometimes they rest a little space on the hind legs and the forefeet crop curling in on the breast, not so liquidly as we see it in the limbs of foals though

Bright afternoon; clear distances; Pendle dappled with tufted shadow; west wind; interesting clouding, flat and lying in the warp of the heaven but the pieces with rounded outline and dolphin-backs shewing in places and all was at odds and at Z's, one piece with another. Later beautifully delicate crisping. Later rippling as in the drawing

April 21—We have had other such afternoons, one today—the sky a beautiful grained blue, silky lingering clouds in flat-bottomed loaves, others a little browner in ropes or in burly-shouldered ridges swanny and lustrous, more in the Zenith stray packs of a sort of violet paleness. White-rose cloud formed fast, not in the same density— some caked and swimming in a wan whiteness, the rest soaked with the blue and like the leaf of a flower held against the light and diapered out by the worm or veining of deeper blue between rosette and rosette. Later / moulding, which brought rain: in perspective it was vaulted in very regular ribs with fretting between: but these are not ribs; they are a "wracking" install made of these two realities—the frets, which are scarves of rotten cloud bellying upwards and drooping at their ends and shaded darkest at the brow or tropic where they double to the eye, and the whiter field of sky shewing between: the illusion looking down the "waggon" is complete. These swaths of fretted cloud move in rank, not in file

April 22—But such a lovely damasking in the sky as today I never felt before. The blue was charged with simple instress, the higher, zenith sky earnest and frowning, lower more light and sweet. High up again, breathing through woolly coats of cloud or on the quains and branches of the flying pieces it was the true exchange of crimson, nearer the earth / against the sun / it was turquoise, and in the opposite south-western bay below the sun it was like clear oil but just as full of colour, shaken over with slanted flashing "travellers," all in flight, stepping one behind the other, their edges tossed with bright ravelling, as if white napkins were thrown up in the sun but not quite at the same moment so that they were all in a scale down the air falling one after the other to the ground

April 27—Went to see Sauley Abbey (Cistercian): there is little to see

Mesmerised a duck with chalk lines drawn from her beak sometimes level and sometimes forwards on a black table. They explain that the bird keeping the abiding offscape of the hand grasping her neck fancies she is still held down and cannot lift her head as long as she looks at the chalk line, which she associates with the power that holds her. This duck lifted her head at once when I put it down on the table without chalk. But this seems inadequate. It is most likely the fascinating instress of the straight white stroke

May 9—A simple behaviour of the cloudscape I have not realised before. Before a N.E. wind great bars or rafters of cloud all the morning and in a manner all the day marching across the sky in regular rank and with equal spaces between. They seem prism-shaped, flat-bottomed and banked up to a ridge: their make is like light tufty snow in coats

This day and May 11 the bluebells in the little wood between the College and the highroad and in one of the Hurst Green cloughs. In the little wood / opposite the light / they stood in blackish spreads or sheddings like the spots on a snake. The heads are then like thongs and solemn in grain and grape-colour. But in the clough / through the light / they came in falls of sky-colour washing the brows and slacks of the ground with vein-blue, thickening at the double, vertical themselves and the young grass and brake fern combed vertical, but the brake struck the upright of all this with light winged transomes. It was a lovely sight.—The bluebells in your hand baffle you with their inscape, made to every sense: if you draw your fingers through them they are lodged and struggle / with a shock of wet heads; the long stalks rub and click and flatten to a fan on one another like your fingers themselves would when you passed the palms hard across one another, making a brittle rub and jostle like the noise of a hurdle strained by leaning against; then there is the faint honey smell and in the mouth the sweet gum when you bite them. But this is easy, it is the eye they baffle. They give one a fancy of panpipes and of some wind instrument with stops—a trombone perhaps. The overhung necks—for growing they are little more than a staff with a simple crook but in water, where they stiffen, they take stronger turns, in the head like sheephooks or, when more waved throughout, like the waves riding through a whip that is being smacked—what with these overhung necks and what with the crisped ruffled bells dropping mostly on one side and the gloss these have at their footstalks they have an air of the knights at chess. Then the knot or "knoop" of buds some shut, some just gaping, which makes the pencil of the whole spike, should be noticed: the inscape of the flower most finely carried out in the siding of the axes, each striking a greater and greater slant, is finished in these clustered buds, which for the most part are not straightened but rise to the end like a tongue and this and their tapering and a little flattening they have make them look like the heads of snakes

May 17 etc—I have several times seen the peacock with train spread lately. It has a very regular warp, like a shell, in which the bird embays himself, the bulge being inwards below but the hollow inwards above, cooping him in and only opening towards the brim, where the feathers are beginning to rive apart. The eyes, which lie alternately when the train is shut, like scales or gadroons, fall into irregular rows when it is opened, and then it thins and darkens against the light, it loses the moistness and satin it has when in the pack but takes another / grave and expressive splendour, and the outermost eyes, detached and singled, give with their corner fringes the suggestion of that inscape of the flowing cusped trefoil which is often effective in art. He shivers it when he first rears it and then again at intervals and when this happens the rest blurs and the eyes start forward.—I have thought it looks like a tray or green basket or fresh-cut willow hurdle set all over with Paradise fruits cut through—first through a beard of golden fibre and then through wet flesh greener than greengages or purpler than grapes—or say that the knife had caught a tatter or flag of the skin and laid it flat across the flesh—and then within all a sluggish corner drop of black or purple oil

On Whit Monday (May 29) went to Preston to see the procession. Though not very splendid it moved me. But just as it was beginning we heard the news of the murder of the hostages by the Commune at the entry of the Government troops into Paris—64 in all, including the Archbishop, Mgr. Maret bishop of Sura, the Curé of the Madeleine, and Fr. Olivain with four other of our Fathers. It was at the same time the burning of the Tuileries and the other public buildings was carried out

[1872]

Feb. 23—A lunar halo: I looked at it from the upstairs library window. It was a grave grained sky, the strands rising a little from left to right. The halo was not quite round, for in the first place it was a little pulled and drawn below, by the refraction of the lower air perhaps, but what is more it fell in on the nether left hand side to rhyme the moon itself, which was not quite at full. I could not but strongly feel in my fancy the odd instress of this, the moon leaning on her side, as if fallen back, in the cheerful light floor within the ring, after with magical rightness and success tracing round her the ring the steady copy of her own outline. But this sober grey darkness and pale light was happily broken through by the orange of the pealing of Mitton bells

Another night from the gallery window I saw a brindled heaven, the moon just marked by a blue spot pushing its way through the darker cloud, underneath and on the skirts of the rack bold long flakes whitened and swaled like feather, below / the garden with the heads of the trees and shrubs furry grey. I read a broad careless inscape flowing throughout

At the beginning of March they were felling some of the ashes in our grove

[1873]

Feb. 24—In the snow flat-topped hillocks and shoulders outlined with wavy edges, ridge below ridge, very like the grain of wood in line and in projection like relief maps. These the wind makes I think and of course drifts, which are in fact snow waves. The sharp nape of a drift is sometimes broken by slant flutes or channels. I think this must be when the wind after shaping the drift first has changed and cast waves in the body of the wave itself. All the world is full of inscape and chance left free to act falls into an order as well as purpose: looking out of my window I caught in the random clods and broken heaps of snow made by the cast of a broom. The same of the path trenched by footsteps in ankledeep snow across the fields leading to Hodder wood through which we went to see the river. The sun was bright, the broken brambles and all boughs and banks limed and cloyed with white, the brook down the clough pulling its way by drops and by bubbles in turn under a shell of ice

In March there was much snow

May 11—Bluebells in Hodder wood, all hanging their heads one way. I caught as well as I could while my companions talked the Greek rightness of their beauty, the lovely / what people call / "gracious" bidding one to another or all one way, the level or stage or shire of colour they make hanging in the air a foot above the grass, and a notable glare the eye may abstract and sever from the blue colour / of light beating up from so many glassy heads, which like water is good to float their deeper instress in upon the mind

May 30—The swifts round and scurl under the clouds in the sky: light streamers were about; the swifts seemed rather to hang and be at rest and to fling these away row by row behind them like spokes of a lighthung wheel

June 5 etc—The turkey and hens will let a little chick mount their backs and sit between the wings

June 15—Sunday after Corpus Christi. Some of us went to Billington to join in their procession. Mr. Lucas was with me. The day was very beautiful. A few streamer clouds and a grapy yellowing team moving along the horizon. At the ferry a man said "Hāst a penny, Tom?"—the old ferry was below the rocks

June 16—Still brighter and warmer, southern-like. Shadows sharp in the quarry and on the shoulders of our two young white pigeons. There is some charm about a thing such as these pigeons or trees when they dapple their boles in wearing its own shadow. I was on the fells with Mr. Strappini. They were all melled and painted with colour and full of roaming scents, and winged silver slips of young brake rising against the light trim and symmetrical and gloried from within reminded me of I do not remember what detail of coats of arms, perhaps the lilies of Eton College. Meadows smeared yellow with buttercups and bright squares of rapefield in the landscape. Fine-weather bales of cloud. Napkin folds brought out on the Parlick ridge and capfuls of shadow in them. A cuckoo flew by with a little bird after it as we lay in the quarry at Kemble End

As I passed the stables later and stayed to look at the peacocks John Myerscough came out to shew me a brood of little peafowl (though it could not be found at that time) and the kindness touched my heart

I looked at the pigeons down in the kitchen yard and so on. They look like little gay jugs by shape when they walk, strutting and jod-jodding with their heads. The two young ones are all white and the pins of the folded wings, quill pleated over quill, are like crisp and shapely cuttle-shells found on the shore. The others are dull thundercolour of black-grape-colour except in the white pieings, the quills and tail, and in the shot of the neck. I saw one up on the eaves of the roof: as it moved its head a crush of satin green came and went, a wet or soft flaming of the light

July 22—Very hot, though the wind, which was south, dappled very sweetly on one's face and when I came out I seemed to put it on like a gown as a man puts on the shadow he walks into and hoods or hats himself with the shelter of a roof, a penthouse, or a copse of trees, I mean it rippled and fluttered like light linen, one could feel the folds and braids of it—and indeed a floating flag is like wind visible and what weeds are in a current; it gives it thew and fires it and bloods it in.—Thunderstorm in the evening, first booming in gong-sounds, as at Aosta, as if high up and so not reechoed from the hills; the lightning very slender and nimble and as if playing very near but after supper it was so bright and terrible some people said they had never seen its like. People were killed, but in other parts of the country it was more violent than with us. Flashes lacing two clouds above or the cloud and the earth started upon the eyes in live veins of rincing or riddling liquid white, inched and jagged as if it were the shivering of a bright riband string which had once been kept bound round a blade and danced back into its pleatings. Several strong thrills of light followed the flash but a grey smother of darkness blotted the eyes if they had seen the fork, also dull furry thickened scapes of it were left in them

Letters

18 New Inn Hall Street, Oxford.
St. Theresa (15 Oct.) 1866.

Very Reverend Father,

I have been up at Oxford just long enough to have heard fr. my father and mother in return for my letter announcing my conversion. Their answers are terrible: I cannot read them twice. If you will pray for them and me just now I shall be deeply thankful. But what I am writing for is this—they urge me with the utmost entreaties to wait till I have taken my degree—more than half a year. Of course it is impossible, and since it is impossible to wait as long as they wish it seems to me useless to wait at all. Wd. you therefore wish me to come to Birmingham at once, on Thursday, Friday, or Saturday? You will understand why I have any hesitation at all, namely because if immediately after their letters urging a long delay I am received without any, it will be another blow and look like intentional cruelty. I did not know till last night the rule about *communicatio in sacris*[8]—at least as binding catechumens, but I now see the alternative thrown open, either to live without Church and sacraments or else, in order to avoid the Catholic Church, to have to attend constantly the services of that very Church. This brings the matter to an absurdity and makes me think that any delay, whatever relief it may be to my parents, is impossible. I am asking you then whether I shall at all costs be received at once.

Strange to say of four conversions mine is the earliest and yet my reception will be last. I think I said that my friend William Garrett was converted and received shortly after hearing of my conversion;

[8]Rule forbidding Catholics to cooperate in worship with non-Catholics.

just before term began another friend, Alexander Wood, wrote to me in perplexity, and when I wrote back to his surprise telling him I was a convert he made up his own mind the next morning and is being received today; by a strange chance he met Addis in town and Addis, who had put off all thought of change for a year, was by God's mercy at once determined to see a priest and was received at Bayswater the same evening—Saturday. All our minds you see were ready to go at a touch and it cannot but be that the same is the case with many here. Addis' loss will be deep grief to Dr. Pusey I think: he has known him so long and stayed with him at Chale in a retreat.

I shall ask F. William Neville to open and answer this in your absence.

Monsignor Eyre seemed to say that I ought not to make my confession by means of a paper as I have been used to do. Will you kindly say whether you wd. prefer it so or not?

Believe me, dear Father, your affectionate son in Christ,

Gerard M. Hopkins.

P.S. And if you shd. bid me be received at once will you kindly name the day? The liberality of the college authorities will throw no hindrance in the way.

TO HIS FATHER

Oct. 16. [1866]

My dear Father,

—I must begin with a practical immediate point. The Church strictly forbids all communion in sacred things with non-Catholics. I have only just learnt this, but it prevents me going to chapel, and so yesterday I had to inform the Dean of Chapel. Today the Master sent for me and said he cd. not grant me leave of absence without an application from you. As the College last term passed a resolution admitting Catholics and took a Catholic into residence it has no right to alter its principle in my case. I wish you therefore not to give yourself the pain of making this application, even if you were willing: I am of age moreover and am alone concerned. If you refuse to make the application, the Master explains that he shall lay my case before the common-room. In this case there is very little doubt indeed that the Fellows wd. take the reasonable course and give me leave of absence fr. chapel, and if not, I am quite contented: but in fact I am satisfied as to the course our Fellows will take and the Master will at the last hesitate to lay the matter before them perhaps even. I want you therefore to write at once, if you will,—not to the Master who has no right to ask what he does, but to me, with a refusal: no harm will follow.

The following is the position of things with me. You ask me to suspend my judgment for a long time, or at the very least more than half a year, in other words to stand still for a time. Now to stand still is not possible, thus: I must either obey the Church or disobey. If I disobey, I am not suspending judgment but deciding, namely to take backward steps fr. the grounds I have already come to. To stand still if it were possible might be justifiable, but to go back nothing can justify. I must therefore obey the Church by ceasing to attend any service of the Church of England. If I am to wait then I must either be altogether without services and sacraments, which you will of course know is impossible, or else I must attend the services of the Church—still being unreceived. But what can be more contradictory than, in order to avoid joining the Church, attending the services of that very Church? Three of my friends, whose conversions were later than mine, Garrett, Addis, and Wood, have already been received, but this is by the way. Only one thing remains to be done: I cannot fight against God Who calls me to His Church: if I were to delay and die in the meantime I shd. have no plea why my soul was not forfeit. I have no power in fact to stir a finger: it is God Who makes the decision and not I.

But you do not understand what is involved in asking me to delay and how little good you wd. get from it. I shall hold as a Catholic what I have long held as an Anglican, that literal truth of our Lord's words by which I learn that the least fragment of the consecrated elements in the Blessed Sacrament of the Altar is the whole Body of Christ born of the Blessed Virgin, before which the whole host of saints and angels as it lies on the altar trembles with adoration. This belief once got is the life of the soul and when I doubted it I shd. become an atheist the next day. But, as Monsignor Eyre says, it is a gross superstition unless guaranteed by infallibility. I cannot hold this doctrine confessedly except as a Tractarian or a Catholic: the Tractarian ground I have seen broken to pieces under my feet. What end then can be served by a delay in wh. I shd. go on believing this doctrine as long as I believed in God and shd. be by the fact of my belief drawn by a lasting strain towards the Catholic Church?

About my hastiness I wish to say this. If the question which is the Church of Christ? cd. only be settled by laborious search, a year and ten years and a lifetime are too little, when the vastness of the subject of theology is taken into account. But God must have made his Church such as to attract and convince the poor and unlearned as well as the learned. And surely it is true, though it will sound pride to say it, that the judgment of one who has seen both sides for a week is better than his who has seen only one for a lifetime. I am surprised you shd. say fancy and aesthetic tastes have led me to my present state of mind: these wd. be better satisfied in the Church of England, for bad taste is always meeting one in the accessories of Catholicism. My conversion is due to the following reasons mainly (I have put them down without order)—(i) simple and strictly drawn arguments partly my own, partly others', (ii) common sense, (iii) reading the Bible, especially the Holy Gospels, where texts like "Thou art Peter" (the evasions proposed for this alone are enough to make one a Catholic) and the manifest position of St. Peter among the Apostles so pursued me that at one time I thought it best to stop thinking of them, (iv) an increasing knowledge of the Catholic system (at first under the form of Tractarianism, later in its genuine place), which only wants to be known in order to be loved—its consolations, its marvelous ideal of holiness, the faith and devotion of its children, its multiplicity, its array of saints and martyrs, its consistency and unity, its glowing prayers, the daring majesty of its claims, etc etc. You speak of the claims of the Church of England, but it is to me the strange thing that the Church of England makes no claims: it is true that Tractarians make them for her and find them faintly or only in a few instances borne out for them by her liturgy, and are strongly assailed for their extravagances while they do it. Then about applying to Mr. Liddon and the Bp. of Oxford. Mr. Liddon writes begging me to pause: it wd. take too long to explain how I did not apply to him at first and why it wd. have been useless. If Dr. Pusey is in Oxford tomorrow I will see him, if it is any satisfaction to you. The Bishop is too much engaged to listen to individual difficulties and those who do apply to him may get such answers as young Mr. Lane Fox did, who gave up £30,000 a year just lately to become a Catholic. He wrote back about a cob which he wanted to sell to the Dean of some place and wh. Lane Fox was to put his own price on and ride over for the Bishop to the place of sale. In fact Dr. Pusey and Mr. Liddon were the only two men in the world who cd. avail to detain me: the fact that they were Anglicans kept me one, for arguments for the Church of England I had long ago felt there were none that wd. hold water, and when that influence gave way everything was gone.

You are so kind as not to forbid me your house, to which I have no claim, on condition, if I understand, that I promise not to try to convert my brothers and sisters. Before I can promise this I must get permission, wh. I have no doubt will be given. Of course this promise will not apply after they come of age. Whether after my reception you will still speak as you do now I cannot tell.

You ask me if I have had no thought of the estrangement. I have had months to think of everything. Our Lord's last care on the cross was to commend His mother to His Church and His Church to His mother in the person of St. John. If even now you wd. put yourselves into that position wh. Christ so unmistakeably gives us and ask the Mother of sorrows to remember her three hours' compassion at the cross, the piercing of the sword prophecied by Simeon, and her seven dolours, and her spouse Joseph, the lily of chastity, to remember the flight into Egypt, the searching for his Foster-Son at twelve years old, and his last ecstacy with Christ at his death-bed, the prayers of this Holy Family wd. in a few days put an end to estrangements for ever. If you shrink fr. doing this, though the Gospels cry aloud to you to do it, at least for once—if you like, only once—approach Christ in a new way in which you will at all events feel that you are exactly in unison with me, that is, not vaguely, but casting yourselves into His sacred broken Heart and His five adorable Wounds. Those who do not pray to Him in His Passion pray to God but scarcely to Christ. I have the right to propose this, for I have tried both ways, and if you will not give one trial to this way you will see you are prolonging the estrangement and not I.

After saying this I feel lighter-hearted, though I still can by no means make my pen write what I shd. wish. I am your loving son,

Gerard M. Hopkins.
23 New Inn Hall Street,
Oct. 17, 1866.

P.S. I am most anxious that you shd. not think of my future. It is likely that the positions you wd. like to see me in wd. have no attraction for me, and surely the happiness of my prospects depends on the happiness to me and not on intrinsic advantages. It is possible even to be very sad and very happy at once and the time that I was with Bridges, when my anxiety came to its height, was I believe the happiest fortnight of my life. My only strong wish is to be independent.

If you are really willing to make the application to the Master, well and good; but I do not want you to put yourself to pain. I have written a remonstrance to him.

Many thanks to Arthur[9] for his letter.

TO ROBERT BRIDGES

St. Beuno's, St. Asaph.
Aug. 21 1877.

Dearest Bridges,

—Your letter cannot amuse Father Provincial, for he is on the unfathering deeps outward bound to Jamaica: I shd. not think of telling you anything about his reverence's goings and comings if it were it [*sic*] not that I know this fact has been chronicled in the Catholic papers.

Enough that it amuses me, especially the story about Wooldridge and the Wagnerite, wh. is very good.

Your parody reassures me about your understanding the metre. Only remark, as you say that there is no conceivable licence I shd. not be able to justify, that with all my licences, or rather laws, I am stricter than you and I might say than anybody I know. With the exception of the *Bremen* stanza, which was, I think, the first written after 10 years' interval of silence, and before I had fixed my principles, my rhymes are rigidly good—to the ear—and such rhymes as *love* and *prove* I scout utterly. And my quantity is not like "Fĭftytwō Bĕdfŏrd Squāre," where *fĭftȳ* might pass but *Bĕdfŏrd* I should never admit. Not only so but Swinburne's dactyls and anapaests are halting

[9]Hopkins's younger brother.

to my ear: I never allow e.g. *I* or *my* (that is diphthongs, for $I=a+i$ and $my=ma=i$) in the short or weak syllables of those feet, excepting before vowels, semi-vowels, or *r*, and rarely then, or when the measure becomes (what is the word?) molossic—thus: $\cup-\cup|\cup-\cup|\cup-\cup$, for then the first short is almost long. If you look again you will see. So that I may say my apparent licences are counterbalanced, and more, by my strictness. In fact all English verse, except Milton's, almost, offends me as "licentious." Remember this.

I do not of course claim to have invented *sprung rhythms* but only *sprung rhythm;* I mean that single lines and single instances of it are not uncommon in English and I have pointed them out in lecturing—e.g. "why should this : desert be?"—which the editors have variously amended; "There to meet: with Macbeth" or "There to meet with Mac : beth"; Campbell has some throughout the *Battle of the Baltic*—"and their fleet along the deep : proudly shone"—and *Ye Mariners*—"as ye sweep : through the deep" etc; . . . and, not to speak of *Pom pom,* in Nursery Rhymes, Weather Saws, and Refrains they are very common—but what I do in the *Deutschland* etc is to enfranchise them as a regular and permanent principle of scansion.

There are no outriding feet in the *Deutschland.* An outriding foot is, by a sort of contradiction, a recognized extra-metrical effect; it is and it is not part of the metre; not part of it, not being counted, but part of it by producing a calculated effect which tells in the general success. But the long, e.g. seven-syllabled, feet of the *Deutschland,* are strictly metrical. Outriding feet belong to counterpointed verse, which supposes a well-known and unmistakable or unforgettable standard rhythm: the *Deutschland* is not counterpointed; counterpoint is excluded by sprung rhythm. But in some of my sonnets I have mingled the two systems: this is the most delicate and difficult business of all.

The choruses in *Samson Agonistes* are intermediate between counterpointed and sprung rhythm. In reality they are sprung, but Milton keeps up a fiction of counterpointing the heard rhythm (which is the same as the mounted rhythm) upon a standard rhythm which is never heard but only counted and therefore really does not exist. The want of a metrical notation and the fear of being thought to write mere rhythmic or (who knows what the critics might not have said?) even unrhythmic prose drove him to this. Such rhythm as French and Welsh poetry has is sprung, counterpointed upon a counted rhythm, but it differs from Milton's in being little calculated, not more perhaps than prose consciously written rhythmically, like orations for instance; it is in fact the *native rhythm* of the words used bodily imported into verse; whereas Milton's mounted rhythm is a real poetical rhythm, having its own laws and recurrence, but further embarrassed by having to count.

Why do I employ sprung rhythm at all? Because it is the nearest to the rhythm of prose, that is the native and natural rhythm of speech, the least forced, the most rhetorical and emphatic of all possible rhythms, combining as it seems to me, opposite and, one wd. have thought, incompatible excellences, markedness of rhythm—that is rhythm's self—and naturalness of expression—for why, if it is forcible in prose to say "lashed : rod," am I obliged to weaken this in verse, which ought to be stronger, not weaker, into "láshed birch-ród" or something?

My verse is less to be read than heard, as I have told you before; it is oratorical, that is the rhythm is so. I think if you will study what I have here said you will be much more pleased with it and may I say? converted to it.

You ask me may you call it "presumptious jugglery." No, but only for this reason, that *presumptious* is not English.

I cannot think of altering anything. Why shd. I? I do not write for the public. You are my public and I hope to convert you.

You say you wd. not for any money read my poem again. Nevertheless I beg you will. Besides money, you know, there is love. If it is obscure do not bother yourself with the meaning but pay attention to the best and most intelligible stanzas, as the two last of each part and the narrative of the wreck. If you had done this you wd. have liked it better and sent me some serviceable criticisms, but now your criticism is of no use, being only a protest memorialising me against my whole policy and proceedings.

I may add for your greater interest and edification that what refers to myself in the poem is all strictly and literally true and did all occur; nothing is added for poetical padding.

Believe me your affectionate friend

Gerard M. Hopkins S.J.

TO ROBERT BRIDGES

Stonyhurst, Blackburn.
May 30 1878.

Dearest Bridges,

—It gave me of course great comfort to read your words of praise. But however, praise or blame, never mingle with your criticisms monstrous and indecent spiritual compliments like something you have said there.

I want to remark on one or two things.

How are hearts of oak furled? Well, in sand and sea water. The image comes out true under the circumstances, otherwise it could not hold together. You are to suppose a stroke or blast in a forest of "heart of oak" (=, ad propositum, sound oak-timber) which at one blow both lays them low and buries them in broken earth. *Furling* (*ferrule* is a blunder for *furl,* I think) is *proper* when said of sticks and staves.

So too of *bole,* I don't see your objection here at all. It is not only used by poets but seems technical and *proper* and in the mouth of timber merchants and so forth.

"This was that fell capsize" is read according to the above stresses—two cretics, so to say.

I don't see the difficulty about the "lurch forward"? Is it in the scanning? which is imitative as usual—an anapaest, followed by a trochee, a dactyl, and a syllable, so that the rhythm is anacrustic or, as I should call it, "encountering."

"Cheer's death" = the death of cheer = the dying out of all comfort = despair.

"It is even seen"—You mistake the sense of this as I feared it would be mistaken. I believed Hare to be a brave and conscientious man: what I say is that "even" those who seem unconscientious will act the right part at a great push.

About "mortholes" I do wince a little but can not now change it. What I dislike much more however is the rhyme "foot he" to *duty* and *beauty.* In fact I cannot stand it and I want the stanza corrected thus—

> Look, foot to forelock, how all things suit! he
> Is strung by duty, is strained to beauty,
>   And brown-as-dawning-skinned
> With brine and shine and whirling wind.

The difficulty about the Milky Way is perhaps because you do not know the allusion: it is that in Catholic times Walsingham Way was a name for the Milky Way, as being supposed a fingerpost to our Lady's shrine at Walsingham.

"O well wept" should be written asunder, not "wellwept." It means "you do well to weep" and is framed like "well caught" or "well run" at a cricketmatch.

Obscurity I do and will try to avoid so far as is consistent with excellences higher than clearness at a first reading. This question of obscurity we will some time speak of but not now. As for affectation I do not believe I am guilty of it: you should point out instances, but as long as mere novelty and boldness strikes you as affectation your criticism strikes me as—as water of the Lower Isis.

I see I have omitted one or two things. If the first stanza is too sudden it can be changed back to what it was at first—

> The Eurydice—it concerned thee, O Lord:
>
> 4   5   1   2   3
> O alas! Three hundred hearts on board

But then it will be necessary to change the third stanza as follows, which you will hardly approve—

> Did she pride her, freighted fully, on
> Bounden bales or a hoard of bullion?—

About "grimstone" you are mistaken. It is not the remains of a rhyme to *brimstone*. I *could* run you some rhymes on it. You must know, we have a Father Grimstone in our province.

I shall never have leisure or desire to write much. There is one thing I should like to get done; an ode on the Vale of Clwyd begun therein. It would be a curious work if done. It contains metrical attempts other than any you have seen, something like Greek choruses, a peculiar eleven-footed line for instance.

What you have got of mine you may do as you like with about shewing to friends.

Is your own ode on Eurydice done? Will you send it, as well as other things; which shall be returned.

Believe me your affectionate friend

Gerard M. Hopkins S.J.

You are kind enough to want me to dine with you on coming up to town. I should have to go to our house at once. I shall have, no doubt, little time when in London but still we shall manage to meet.

TO ROBERT BRIDGES

Oct. 25 [1879]

. . . I think then no one can admire beauty of the body more than I do, and it is of course a comfort to find beauty in a friend or a friend in beauty. But this kind of beauty is dangerous. Then comes the beauty of the mind, such as genius, and this is greater than the beauty of the body and not to call dangerous. And more beautiful than the beauty of the mind is beauty of character, the "handsome heart." Now every beauty is not a wit or genius nor has every wit or genius character. For though even bodily beauty, even the beauty of blooming health, is from the soul, in the sense, as we Aristotelian Catholics say, that the soul is the form of the body, yet soul may have no other beauty, so to speak, than that which it expresses in the symmetry of the body—barring those blurs in the cast which wd. not be found in the die or the mould. This needs no illustration, as all know it. But what is more to be remarked is that in like manner the soul may have no further beauty than that which is seen in the mind, that there may be genius uninformed by character. I sometimes wonder at this in a man like Tennyson: his gift of utterance is truly golden, but go further home and you come to thoughts commonplace and wanting in nobility (it seems hard to say it but I think you know what I mean). In Burns there is generally recognized on the other hand a richness and beauty of manly character which lends worth to some of his smallest fragments, but there is a great want in his utterance; it is never really beautiful, he had no eye for pure beauty, he gets no nearer than the fresh picturesque expressed in fervent and flowing language (the most strictly beautiful lines of his that I remember are those in Tam o' Shanter: "But pleasures are like poppies spread" sqq. and those are not). Between a fineness of nature which wd. put him in the first rank of writers and a poverty of language which puts him in the lowest rank of poets, he takes to my mind, when all is balanced and cast up, about a middle place. . . .

TO R. W. DIXON

Manresa House, Roehampton, London, S.W.
(By the by have you read Lothair?[10] because this house is the divine Theodora's: some of the scenes are laid here.)

Oct. 12 1881.

My dear Friend,
—Some of the sonnets are very, I must say unpardonably, licentious in form. I recognize stricter and looser forms and the Shakespearian [*sic*] sonnet, though it is a sonnet only *in genere* and not one if by sonnet you mean the Italian sonnet, which is the sonnet proper—but this is a question of names only—the Shakespearian sonnet is a very beautiful and effective species of composition in the kind. But then, though simpler, it is as strict, regular, and specific as the sonnet proper. Moreover it has the division into the parts 8+6, at all events 4+4+4+2. Now it seems to me that this division is the real characteristic of the sonnet and that what is not so marked off and more-

---

[10]*Lothair* (1870), a novel by Benjamin Disraeli, whose heroine was Theodora.

over has not the octet again divided into quatrains is not to be called a sonnet at all. For in the cipher 14 is no mystery and if one does not know nor avail oneself of the opportunities which it affords it is a pedantic encumbrance and not an advantage. The equation of the best sonnet is

$$(4+4) + (3+3) = 2.4 + 2.3 = 2(4+3) + 2.7 = 14.$$

This means several things—(A) that the sonnet is one of the works of art of which the equation or construction is unsymmetrical in the shape $x+y = a$, where x and y are unequal in some simple ratio, as 2:1, 3:2, 4:3: perhaps it would be better to say $mx = nx = a$. Samples of this are the Hexameter and Ionic Trimeter, divided by their caesura, as St. Austin *De Musica* suggests, so as to give the equation $3^2 + 4^2 = 5^2$ (it is not very clear how he makes it out, but at all events they give the equation $2\frac{1}{2} + 3\frac{1}{2} = 6$ or $5+7 = 12$). The major and minor scales again consist of a pentachord $+$ a tetrachord and in Plainsong music all the "Authentic" Modes have this order and all the "Plagal" the reverse, the tetrachord first. And I could shew, if there were time, that it would be impracticable to have a ratio of the sort required with numbers higher than 4 and 3. Neither would 4:2 do, for it wd. return to 2:1, which is too simple. (B) It is divided symmetrically too in multiples of two, as in all effects taking place in time tend to be, and all very regular musical composition is: this raises the 7 to 14. (C) It pairs off even symmetrical members with symmetrical (the quatrains) and the uneven or unsymmetrical with uneven (the tercets). And even the rhymes, did time allow, I could shew are founded on a principle of nature and cannot be altered without loss of effect. But when one goes so far as to run the rhymes of the octet into the sestet a downright prolapsus or hernia takes place and the sonnet is crippled for life.

I have been longer and perhaps more dogmatic than I shd. have been over this point. Of the sonnets themselves those on the World, except for happy touches, do not interest me very much and that to Corneille has a certain stiffness, as the majority of Wordsworth's have, great sonneteer as he was, but he wrote in "Parnassian," that is the language and style of poetry mastered and at command but employed without any fresh inspiration: and this I feel of your sonnet here. The rest, that to George Sand and those on Shakespeare and Milton, are rich in thought, feeling, and diction.

On a Young Bird etc.—This is a truly touching and finished little piece, the tale told with great flow and simplicity: the pathos of a little tale like this is unique as a well-told jest and has its own point as that has. There are however two flaws worth noticing. It seems strange and, I think, unlawful to call a "naked floor" a bower: a bower is a *camera,* an arched shelter whether of boughs or of cieling [*sic*]. Also stanza 4. begins with rhyme as 3. ends with, which is an awkwardness.

Ode on the Death of Dickens is fine and stirring; the Aryan image of the cloud cows and the dog particularly striking; but the anapaests are heavily loaded. For myself I have been accustomed to think, as many critics do, that Dickens had no true command of pathos, that in his there is something mawkish; but perhaps I have not read the best passages. Just such a gale as this poem paints is blowing today (Oct. 14) and two of my fellow Tertians have been injured by the fall of almost half a tall cedar near my room, which wrecked the woodshed where they happened to be and battered and bruised them with a rain of tiles.

The Fall of the Leaf—I have spoken of this beautiful poem before.

I cannot remember if I spoke of *Nature and Man,* the one beginning "Blue in the mists all day." At all events it is one of the most perfect of all, both in thought and expression. The thing had to be said. I suppose "pod" means some pod-like bud, for I think, scientifically speaking, the pod is only a seed vessel.

There only remain the two tales; of which I will write another day, though it must be less fully than they deserve. I will finish with remarks called out by your most welcome letter of yesterday.

In speaking of "frigid fancy" I referred to the particular passage only. But Browning has, I think, many frigidities. Any untruth to nature, to human nature, is frigid. Now he has got a great deal of what came in with Kingsley and the Broad Church school, a way of talking (and making his people talk) with the air and spirit of a man bouncing up from table with his mouth full of bread and cheese and saying that he meant to stand no blasted nonsense. There is a whole volume of Kingsley's essays which is all a kind of munch and a not standing of any blasted nonsense from cover to cover. Do you know what I mean? The *Flight of the Duchess,* with the repetition of "My friend," is in this vein. Now this is *one* mood or vein of human nature, but they would have it all and look at all human nature through it. And Tennyson in his later works has been "carried away with their dissimulation." The effect of this style is a frigid bluster. A true humanity of spirit, neither mawkish on the one hand nor blustering on the other, is the most precious of all qualities in style, and this I prize in your poems, as I do in Bridges'. After all it is the breadth of his human nature that we admire in Shakespeare.

I read some, not much, of the *Ring and the Book,* but as the tale was not edifying and one of our people, who had been reviewing it, said that further on it was coarser, I did not see, without a particular object, sufficient reason for going on with it. So far as I read I was greatly struck with the skill in which he displayed the facts from different points of view: this is masterly, and to do it through three volumes more shews a great body of genius. I remember a good case of "the impotent collection of particulars" of which you speak in the description of the market place at Florence where he found the book of the trial: it is a pointless photograph of still life, such as I remember in Balzac, minute upholstery description; only that in Balzac, who besides is writing prose, all tells and is given with a reserve and simplicity of style which Browning has not got. Indeed I hold with the old-fashioned criticism that Browning is not really a poet, that he has all the gifts but the one needful and the pearls without the string; rather one should say raw nuggets and rough diamonds. I suppose him to resemble Ben Jonson, only that Ben Jonson has more real poetry.

As for Carlyle; I have a letter by me never sent, in answer to a pupil of mine, who had written about him, and I find I there say just what you do about his incapacity of general truths. And I always thought him morally an imposter, worst of all imposters a false prophet. And his style has imposture or pretence in it. But I find it difficult to think there is imposture in his genius itself. However I must write no more criticism.

I see you do not understand my position in the Society. This Tertianship or Third Year of Probation or second Noviceship, for it is variously called in the Institute, is not really a noviceship at all in the sense of a time during which a candidate or probationer makes trial of our life and is free to withdraw. At the end of the noviceship proper we take vows which are perpetually binding and renew them every six months (not *for* every six months but for life) till we are professed or take the final degree we are to hold, of which in the Society there are several. It is in preparation for these last vows that we make the tertianship; which is called a *schola affectus* and is meant to enable us to recover that fervour which may have cooled through application to study and contact with the world. Its exercises are however nearly the same as those of the first noviceship. As for myself, I have not only made my vows publicly some two and twenty times but I make them to myself every day, so that I should be black with perjury if I drew back now. And beyond that I can say with St. Peter: To whom shall I go? *Tu verba vitae asternae habes.*[11] Besides all which, my mind is here more at peace than it has ever been and I would gladly live all my life, if it were so to be, in as great or a greater seclusion from the world and be busied only with God. But in the midst of outward occupations not only the mind is drawn away from God, which may be at the call of duty and be God's will, but unhappily the will too is entangled, worldly interests freshen, and worldly ambitions revive. The man who in the world is as dead to the world as if he were buried in the cloister is already a saint. But this is our ideal.

Our Rector Fr. Morris shd. be known to you as a historian in your own field and epoch of history.

Believe me your affectionate friend

Gerard M. Hopkins S.J.

TO R. W. DIXON

(29 October 1881)

I am ashamed at the expressions of high regard which your last letter and others have contained, kind and touching as they are, and do not know whether I ought to reply to them or not. This I say: my vocation puts before me a standard so high that a higher can be found nowhere else. The question then for me is not whether I am willing (if I may guess what is in your mind) to make a sacrifice of hopes of fame (let us suppose), but whether I am not to undergo a severe judgment from God for the lothness I have shewn in making it, for the reserves I may have in my heart made, for the backward glances I have given with my hand upon the plough, for the waste of time

[11]"You have the words of eternal life." John 6:68.

the very compositions you admire may have caused and their preoccupation of the mind which belonged to more sacred or more binding duties, for the disquiet and the thoughts of vainglory they have given rise to. A purpose may look smooth and perfect from without but be frayed and faltering from within. I have never wavered in my vocation, but I have not lived up to it. I destroyed the verse I had written when I entered the Society and meant to write no more; the *Deutschland* I began after a long interval at the chance suggestion of my superior, but that being done it is a question whether I did well to write anything else. However I shall, in my present mind, continue to compose, as occasion shall fairly allow, which I am afraid will be seldom and indeed for some years past has been scarcely ever, and let what I produce wait and take its chance; for a very spiritual man once told me that with things like composition the best sacrifice was not to destroy one's work but to leave it entirely to be disposed of by obedience. But I can scarcely fancy myself asking a superior to publish a volume of my verses and I own that humanly there is very little likelihood of that ever coming to pass. And to be sure if I chose to look at things on one side and not the other I could of course regret this bitterly. But there is more peace and it is the holier lot to be unknown than to be known.—In no case am I willing to write anything while in my present condition: the time is precious and will not return again and I know I shall not regret my forbearance. If I do get hereafter any opportunity of writing poetry I could find it in my heart to finish a tragedy of which I have a few dozen lines written and the leading thoughts for the rest in my head on the subject of St. Winefred's martyrdom: as it happens, tomorrow is her feastday.

TO R. W. DIXON

Manresa House, Roehampton, S.W.

Dec. 1 1881

(the very day 300 years ago of Father Campion's[12] martyrdom).

My dear friend,

—I am heartily glad you did not make away with, as you say you thought of doing, so warm and precious a letter as your last. It reached me on the first break or day of repose in our month's retreat; I began answering it on the second, but could not finish; and this is the third and last of them.

When a man has given himself to God's service, when he has denied himself and followed Christ, he has fitted himself to receive and does receive from God a special guidance, a more particular providence. This guidance is conveyed partly by the action of other men, as his appointed superiors, and partly by direct lights and inspirations. If I wait for such guidance, through whatever channel conveyed, about anything, about my poetry for instance, I do more wisely in every way than if I try to serve my own seeming interests in the matter. Now if you value what I write, if I do myself, much more does our Lord. And if he chooses to avail himself of what I leave at his disposal he can do so with a felicity and with a success which I could never command. And if he does not, then two things follow; one that the reward I shall nevertheless receive from him will be all the greater; the other that then I shall know how much a thing contrary to his will and even to my own best interests I should have done if I had taken things into my own hands and forced on publication. This is my principle and this in the main has been my practice: leading the sort of life I do here it seems easy, but when one mixes with

---

[12]Edmund Campion (1540–81), English Jesuit martyred under Queen Elizabeth. Canonized in 1970.

the world and meets on every side its secret solicitations, to live by faith is harder, is very hard; nevertheless of God's help I shall always do so.

Our Society values, as you say, and has contributed to literature, to culture; but only as a means to an end. Its history and its experience shew that literature proper, as poetry, has seldom been found to be to that end a very serviceable means. We have had for three centuries often the flower of the youth of a country in numbers enter our body: among these how many poets, how many artists of all sorts, there must have been! But there have been very few Jesuit poets and, where they have been, I believe it would be found on examination that there was something exceptional in their circumstances or, so to say, counterbalancing in their career. For genius attracts fame and individual fame St. Ignatius looked on as the most dangerous and dazzling of all attractions ... You see then what is against me, but since, as Solomon says, there is a time for everything, there is nothing that does not some day come to be, it may be that the time will come for my verses. I remember, by the by, once taking up a little book of the life of St. Stanislaus told or commented on under emblems; it was much in the style of Herbert and his school and about that date; it was by some Polish Jesuit. I was astonished at their beauty and brilliancy, but the author is quite obscure. Brilliancy does not suit us. Bourdaloue is reckoned our greatest orator: he is severe in style. Suarez is our most famous theologian: he is a man of vast volume of mind, but without originality or brilliancy; he treats everything satisfactorily, but you never remember a phrase of his, the manner is nothing. Molina is the man who *made* our theology: he was a genius and even in his driest dialectic I have remarked a certain fervour like a poet's. But in the great controversy on the Aids of Grace, the most dangerous crisis, as I suppose, which our Society ever went through till its suppression, though it was from his book that it had arisen, he took, I think, little part. The same sort of thing may be noticed in our saints. St. Ignatius himself was certainly, every one who reads his life will allow, one of the most extraordinary men that ever lived; but after the establishment of the Order he lived in Rome so ordinary, so hidden a life, that when after his death they began to move in the process of his canonization one of the Cardinals, who had known him in his later life and in that way only, said that he had never remarked anything in him more than in any edifying priest . . . I quote these cases to prove that show and brilliancy do not suit us, that we cultivate the commonplace outwardly and wish the beauty of the king's daughter the soul to be from within.

I could say much more on all this, but it is enough and I must go on to other things. Our retreat ended on the 8th. The "hoity toity" passage I have not seen; indeed I have never even had your book in my hands except one day when waiting to see Bridges in his sickness I found it on the table and was just going to open it—but to the best of my remembrance I did not then open it either. I have for some years past had to put aside serious study. It is true if I had been where your book was easy of access I should have looked at it, perhaps read it all, but in Liverpool I never once entered the public library. However if, as I hope, the time for reading history should ever come I shall try to read this one. You said once you did not pretend not to have a side and that you must write as an Anglican: this is of course and you could not honestly be an Anglican and not write as one . . . My Liverpool and Glasgow experience laid upon my mind a conviction, a truly crushing conviction, of the misery of town life to the poor and more than to the poor, of the misery of the poor in general, of the degradation even of our race, of the hollowness of this century's civilisation: it made even life a burden to me to have daily thrust upon me the things I saw.

I have found to my dismay what I suspected before, that my sister only sent you the music of two stanzas of your Song, whereas I made it for six. How she came to make so dreadful an oversight I cannot tell: the music changes and she had remarked on the change. But I must get her to send the rest and then you will be able to judge of the whole. I do not believe that my airs—if I can compare them with the work of an accomplished musician—would really be found to be like Mr. Metcalf's—to judge by the two pieces of his that you sent me.

I should tell you that I by no means objected to the couplet "Rattled her keys," I admired it as a happy medley: I thought the fusion or rather the pieing was less happy in the opening of the poem.

About sonnet-writing I never meant to override your own judgment. I have put the objections to licentious forms and I believe they hold. But though many sonnets in English may in point of form be great departures from and degenerations of the type, put aside the reference to the type, and they may in themselves be fine poems of 14 lines. Still that fact, that the poet has tied himself within 14 lines and calls the piece a sonnet, lays him open to objection.

I must hold that you and Morris belong to one school, and that though you should neither of you have read a line of the other's. I suppose the same models, the same masters, the same tastes, the same keepings, above all, make the school. It will always be possible to find differences, marked differences, between original minds; it will be necessarily so. So the species in nature are essentially distinct, nevertheless they are grouped into genera: they have one form in common, mounted on that they have a form that differences them. I used to call it the school of Rossetti: it is in literature the school of the Praeraphaelites. Of course that phase is in part past, neither do these things admit of hard and fast lines; still consider yourself, that you know Rossetti and Burne Jones, Rossetti through his sympathy for you and Burne Jones—was it the same or your sympathy for him? This modern medieval school is descended from the Romantic school (Romantic is a bad word) of Keats, Leigh Hunt, Hood, indeed of Scott early in the century. That was one school; another was that of the Lake poets and also of Shelley and Landor; the third was the sentimental school, of Byron, Moore, Mrs. Hemans, and Haynes Bailey. Schools are very difficult to class: the best guide, I think, are keepings. Keats' school chooses medieval keepings, not pure nor drawn from the middle ages direct but as brought down through that Elizabethan tradition of Shakspere and his contemporaries which died out in such men as Herbert and Herrick. They were also great realists and observers of nature. The Lake poets and all that school represent, as it seems to me, the mean or standard of English style and diction, which culminated in Milton but was never very continuous or vigorously transmitted, and in face none of these men unless perhaps Landor were great masters of style, though their diction is generally pure, lucid, and unarchaic. They were faithful but not rich observers of nature. Their keepings are their weak point, a sort of colourless classical keepings: when Wordsworth wants to describe a city or a cloudscape which reminds him of a city it is some ordinary rhetorical stage-effect of domes, palaces, and temples. Byron's school had a deep feeling but the most untrustworthy and barbarous eye, for nature; a diction markedly modern; and their keepings any gaud or a lot of Oriental rubbish. I suppose Crabbe to have been in form a descendant of the school of Pope with a strong and modern realistic eye; Rogers something between Pope's school and that of Wordsworth and Landor; and Campbell between this last and Byron's, with a good deal of Popery too, and a perfect master of style. Now since this time Tennyson and his school seem to me to have struck a mean or compromise between Keats and the medievalists on the one hand and Wordsworth and the Lake School on the other (Tennyson has some jarring notes of Byron in *Lady Clare Vere de Vere, Locksley Hall* and elsewhere). The Lake School expires in Keble and Faber and Cardinal Newman. The Brownings may be reckoned to the Romantics. Swinburne is a strange phenomenon: his poetry seems a powerful effort at establishing a new standard of poetical diction, of the rhetoric of poetry; but to waive every other objection it is essentially archaic, biblical a good deal, and so on: now that is a thing that can never last; a perfect style must be of its age. In virtue of this archaism and on other grounds he must rank with the medievalists.

This is a long ramble on literary matters, on which I did not want to enter.

At Torquay Bridges made at last a sudden and wonderful recovery: so I am told, for he has not written. He then went abroad with a common friend of ours, Muirhead, and is, I suppose, likely to be abroad for the winter. And I am afraid when he returns I shall not see him; for I may now be called away at any time.

Earnestly thanking you for your kindness and wishing you all that is best I remain your affectionate friend

Gerard M. Hopkins S.J.

TO ROBERT BRIDGES

Stonyhurst College,
Blackburn.
Feb. 3 1883.

Dearest Bridges,

I cd. not venture to ask that our library should subscribe half a sovereign for an *édition de luxe* of a new book[13] by an almost unknown author; still less could I expect, nor shd. I like, you to present me, that is our library, with a copy. Here then is a downright deadlock and there is nothing for it but for me to wait for the second edition and then, like Brewer in the *Mutual Friend,* "see how things look."

Many thanks for the anthems. I remember now that I heard the

[13]R. B.'s *Prometheus the Firegiver.*

first at Magdalen. Did you remark that the first 9 notes of the hallelujah are, with a slight change, the beginning of *Cease your funning?* . . .

I quite understand what you mean about gentlemen and "damfools"; it is a very striking thing and I could say much on the subject. I shall not say that much, but I say this: if a gentleman feels that to be what we call a gentleman is a thing essentially higher than without being a gentleman to be ever so great an artist or thinker or if, to put it another way, an artist or thinker feels that were he to become in those ways ever so great he wd. still essentially be lower than a gentleman that was no artist and no thinker—and yet to be a gentleman is but on the brim of morals and rather a thing of manners than of morals properly—then how much more must art and philosophy and manners and breeding and everything else in the world be below the least degree of true virtue. This is that chastity of mind which seems to lie at the very heart and be the parent of all other good, the seeing at once what is best, the holding to that, and the not allowing anything else whatever to be even heard pleading to the contrary. Christ's life and character are such as appeal to all the world's admiration, but there is one insight St. Paul gives us of it which is very secret and seems to me more touching and constraining than everything else is:[14] This mind, he says, was in Christ Jesus—he means as man: being in the form of God—that is, finding, as in the first instant of his incarnation he did, his human nature informed by the godhead—he thought it nevertheless no snatching-matter for him to be equal with God, but annihilated himself, taking the form of servant; that is, he could not but see what he was, God, but he would see it as if he did not see it, and be it as if he were not and instead of snatching at once at what all the time was his, or was himself, he emptied or exhausted himself so far as that was possible, of godhead and behaved only as God's slave, as his creature, as man,

[14]Philippians 2:5–11.

which also he was, and then being in the guise of man humbled himself to death, the death of the cross. It is this holding of himself back, and not snatching at the truest and highest good, the good that was his right, nay his possession from a past eternity in his other nature, his own being and self, which seems to me the root of all his holiness and the imitation of this the root of all moral good in other men. I agree then, and vehemently, that a gentleman, if there is such a thing on earth, is in the position to despise the poet, were he Dante or Shakspere, and the painter, were he Angelo or Apelles, for anything in him that shewed him *not* to be a gentleman. He is in the position to do it, I say, but if he is a gentleman perhaps this is what he will not do. Which leads me to another remark.

The quality of a gentleman is so very fine a thing that it seems to me one should not be at all hasty in concluding that one possesses it. People assume that they have it, take it quite for granted, and claim the acknowledgment from others: now I should say that this also is "no snatching-matter." And the more a man feels what it means and is—and to feel this is certainly some part of it—the more backward he will be to think he can have realized in himself anything so perfect. It is true, there is nothing like the truth and "the good that does itself not know scarce is"; so the perfect gentleman will know that he is the perfect gentleman. But few can be in the position to know this and, being imperfect gentlemen, it will perhaps be a point of their gentlemanliness, for a gentleman is modest, to feel that they are not perfect gentlemen.

By the by if the English race had done nothing else, yet if they left the world the notion of a gentleman, they would have done a great service to mankind.

As a fact poets and men of art are, I am sorry to say, by no means necessarily or commonly gentlemen. For gentlemen do not pander to lust or other basenesses nor, as you say, give themselves airs and affectations nor do other things to be found in modern works. And this adds a charm to everything Canon Dixon writes, that you feel he is a gentleman and thinks like one. But now I have prosed my prose and long enough.

Believe me your affectionate friend

Gerard M. Hopkins S.J.

TO BRIDGES

University College, 85 & 86, Stephens Green, Dublin.

March 7 1884

My dearest Bridges,

—Remark the above address: it is a new departure or a new arrival and at all events a new abode. I dare say you know nothing of it, but the fact is that, though unworthy of and unfit for the post, I have been elected Fellow of the Royal University of Ireland in the department of classics. I have a salary of £400 a year, but when I first contemplated the six examinations I have yearly to conduct, five of them running, and to the Matriculation there came up last year 750 candidates, I thought that Stephen's Green (the biggest square in Europe) paved with gold would not pay for it. It is an honour and an opening and has many bright sides, but at present it has also some dark ones and this in particular that I am not at all strong, not strong enough for the requirements, and do not see at all how I am to become so. But to talk of weather or health and especially to complain of them is poor work.

The house we are in, the College, is a sort of ruin and for purposes of study very nearly naked. And I have more money to buy books than room to put them in.

I have been warmly welcomed and most kindly treated. But Dublin itself is a joyless place and I think in my heart as smoky as

London is: I had fancied it quite different. The Phoenix Park is fine, but inconveniently far off. There are a few fine buildings.

It is only a few days since I sent the MS book to Mr. Patmore (and in packing I mislaid, I hope not lost, your copy of the poem "Wild air, world-mothering air," so that I had to send that unfinished): he acknowledged it this morning.

I enclose a poem of Tennyson's which you may not have seen. It has something in it like your Spring Odes and also some expressions like my sonnet on Spring.

I shall also enclose, if I can find, two triolets I wrote for the Stony-hurst Magazine; for the third was not good, and they spoilt what point it had by changing the title. These two under correction I like, but have fears that you will suspend them from a hooked nose: if you do, still I should maintain they were as good as yours beginning "All women born."

Believe me your affectionate friend

Gerard Hopkins S.J.

There was an Irish row over my election

TO COVENTRY PATMORE

[University College, St. Stephen's Green, Dublin.]
June 4 1886

My dear Mr. Patmore,

—I have been meaning and meaning to write to you, to return the volumes of Barnes's poems you lent me and for other reasons, and partly my approaching examination work restrained me, when last night there reached me from Bell's the beautiful new edition of your works. I call it beautiful and think it is the best form upon the whole for poetry and works of pure literature that I know of and I thank you for your kindness in sending it. And I hope the bush or the bottle may do what little in a bush or bottle lies to recommend the liquor to the born and the unborn. But how slowly does the fame of excellence spread! And crooked eclipses and other obscure causes fight against its rise and progress.

Your poems are a good deed done for the Catholic Church and another for England, for the British Empire, which now trembles in the balance held in the hand of unwisdom. I remark that those Englishmen who wish prosperity to the Empire (which is not all Englishmen or Britons, strange to say) speak of the Empire's mission to extend freedom and civilization in India and elsewhere. The greater the scale of politics the weightier the influence of a great name and a high ideal. It is a terrible element of weakness that now we are not well provided with the name and ideal which would recommend and justify our Empire. "Freedom": it is perfectly true that British freedom is the best, the only successful freedom, but that is because, with whatever drawbacks, those who have developed that freedom have done so with the aid of law and obedience to law. The cry then shd. be Law and Freedom, Freedom and Law. But that does not please: it must be Freedom only. And to that cry there is the telling answer: No freedom you can give us is equal to the freedom of letting us alone: take yourselves out of India, let us first be free of you. Then there is civilisation. It shd. have been Catholic truth. That is the great end of Empires before God, to be Catholic and draw nations into their Catholicism. But our Empire is less and less Christian as it grows. There remains that part of civilisation which is outside Christianity or which is not essentially Christian. The best is gone, still something worth having is left. How far can the civilisation England offers be attractive and valuable and be offered and insisted on as an attraction and a thing of value to India for instance? Of course those who live in our civilisation and belong to it praise it: it is not hard, as Socrates said, among the Athenians to praise the

Athenians; but how will it be represented by critics bent on making the worst of it or even not bent on making the best of it? It is good to be in Ireland to hear how enemies, and those rhetoricians, can treat the things that are unquestioned at home. I know that to mere injustice and slander innocence and excellence themselves stand condemned, but since there is always in mankind some love of truth and admiration for good (only that the truth must be striking and the good on a great scale) what marked and striking excellence has England to shew to make her civilisation attractive? Her literature is one of her excellences and attractions and I believe that criticism will tend to make this more and more felt; but there must be more of that literature, a continued supply and in quality excellent. This is why I hold that fine works of art, and especially if, like yours, that are not only ideal in form but deal with high matter as well, are really a great power in the world, an element of strength even to an empire. But now time and tediousness forbid me to write more on this.

It has struck me since I was at Hastings that, if it is not impertinent of me to say it, Miss Patmore might gain by taking some lessons from some painter. It is true she does what no painter can either do or teach but it is also true there are other things she might with advantage learn. For in fact everyone is the better for teaching: it is universally true. It struck me that she was hampered by want of some mechanical knowledge, as in the use of washes for background, and she tends, I think, to use bodycolour in a way which would be considered vicious. This has naturally arisen from her circumstances; for in the delicate detail in which she so wonderfully excels the use of bodycolour is legitimate and even necessary and naturally she extended a practice with which she was familiar to a new field. I will send Barnes's poems back in a few days.

Believe me your sincere friend

Gerard M. Hopkins S.J.

Please give my kindest remembrances to Mrs. Patmore and the Miss Patmores. I hope all are well and Piff is not killing himself with his sensibilities.

June 6.

TO HIS MOTHER

Written at F. Gerard's dictation.
University College, St. Stephen's Green, Dublin.
May 8. 89

My dearest Mother,

My fever is a sort of typhoid: it is not severe, and my mind has never for a moment wandered. It would give me little pain were it not that while it was incubating I exposed my head to a cold wind, and took neuralgia which torments me now. Thank you for your letters and the flowers which duly revived in water: they are on my table now.

I wonder that none of you understood the allusion to the Garden of Sleep. It is a sentimental song which I thought you must be sick and tired of in England as it has now come over to us. Charlton or Clement Scott is the Author of the words. By every post he receives enquiries as to his meaning which he cannot give except that the Garden of Sleep is a poppy-grown churchyard in the Corner of the Cliff. He gives a text from Ruskin to the effect that all pure natures admire bright colours, referring to the poppies. Accordingly with his genius and his purity he must be a good catch. The Composer is Isidore de Lara who is represented with Byronic look[,] heavy moustaches and furred cloak. He sings his own songs. The piece is not without merit; but when you have heard it as often as I have taken beef tea and chicken jelly, you will have had enough of it.

I had a good deal of sleep last night. The nurse is first rate and every condition is present that could make a serious thing trifling. The only complaint I have to make is that food and medicine keep coming in like cricket balls. I have in fact every attention possible.

Best love to all—I am your affectionate son

Gerard.
per T. W.

Poetics

POETIC DICTION

[AN ESSAY WRITTEN FOR THE MASTER OF BALLIOL 1865 (?)]

Wordsworth's view was that poetic diction scarcely differed or ought to differ from that of prose: he said "The most interesting parts of the best poems will be found to be strictly the language of prose when prose is well written." The protest which his criticisms and to some degree his poetry made against the wide separation existing and believed to exist between the two things was, acting as a corrective, truer for the time than anything which could be said on the other side. His view could not however be received as decisive without more modification than is given in his essay.

If the best prose and the best poetry use the same language— (Coleridge defined poetry as the best thoughts in the best words)— why not use unfettered prose of the two? Because, it would be answered, of the beauty of verse. This is quite insufficient: then bald prose and simple statement would be made better by verse, whereas everyone feels that they are made worse. No, it is plain that metre, rhythm, rhyme, and all the structure which is called verse both necessitate and engender a difference in diction and in thought. The effect of verse is one on expression and on thought, viz. concentration and all which is implied by this. This does not mean terseness nor rejection of what is collateral nor emphasis nor even definiteness though these may be very well, or best, attained by verse, but mainly, though the words are not quite adequate, vividness of idea or, as they would especially have said in the last century, liveliness.

But what the character of poetry is will be found best by looking at the structure of verse. The artificial part of poetry, perhaps we shall be right to say all artifice, reduces itself to the principle of parallelism. The structure of poetry is that of continuous parallelism, ranging from the technical so-called Parallelism of Hebrew poetry and the antiphons of Church music up to the intricacy of Greek or Italian or English verse. But parallelism is of two kinds necessarily— where the opposition is clearly marked, and where it is transitional rather or chromatic. Only the first kind, that of marked parallelism, is concerned with the structure of verse—in rhythm, the recurrence of a certain sequence of rhythm, in alliteration, in assonance and in rhyme. Now the force of this recurrence is to beget a recurrence or parallelism answering to it in the words or thought and, speaking roughly and rather for the tendency than the invariable result, the more marked parallelism in structure whether of elaboration or of emphasis begets more marked parallelism in the words and sense. And moreover parallelism in expression tends to beget or passes into parallelism in thought. This point reached we shall be able to see and account for the peculiarities of poetic diction. To the marked or abrupt kind of parallelism belong metaphor, simile, parable, and so on, where the effect is sought in likeness of things, and antithesis, contrast, and so on, where it is sought in unlikeness. To the chromatic parallelism belong gradation, intensity, climax, tone, expression (as the word is used in music), *chiaroscuro,* perhaps emphasis: while the faculties of Fancy and Imagination might range widely over both kinds, Fancy belonging more especially to the abrupt than to the transitional class.

Accordingly we may modify what Wordsworth says. An emphasis of structure stronger than the common construction of sentences gives asks for an emphasis of expression stronger than that of common speech or writing, and that for an emphasis of thought stronger than that of common thought. And it is commonly supposed that poetry has tasked the highest powers of man's mind: this is because, as it asked for greater emphasis of thought and on a greater scale, at each stage it threw out the minds unequal to further ascent. The diction of poetry could not then be the same with that of prose, and again of prose we can see from the other side that its diction ought not to be that of poetry, and that the great abundance of metaphor or antithesis is displeasing because it is not called for by, and interferes with, the continuousness of its flow. For the necessities or conditions of every act are as Lessing shews the rules by which to try it. And to come to particulars, why for instance, on Wordsworth's principle strictly interpreted, should the accentuation of the last syllable of participles, which so common as it is seems perpetually able to add fresh beauty where it is applied, be used in verse and never in prose? Or in poetry why should it give more pleasure than as being a complement of the mere structural apparatus of verse? as it does in lines like

> So I am as the rich whose blessed key
> Can bring him to his sweet up-lockèd treasure,

It is because where the structure forces us to appreciate each syllable it is natural and in the order of things for us to dwell on all modifications affecting the general result or type which the ear preserves and accordingly with such as are in themselves harmonious we are pleased, but in prose where syllables have none or little determinate value to emphasise them is unmeaning.

"ALL WORDS MEAN EITHER THINGS OR RELATIONS OF THINGS"
[Feb. 9, 1868]

All words mean either things or relations of things: you may also say then substances or attributes or again wholes or parts. Eg., *man* and *quarter.*

To every word meaning a thing and not a relation belongs a passion or prepossession or enthusiasm which it has the power of suggesting or producing but not always or in every one. This *not always* refers to its evolution in the man and secondly in man historically.

The latter element may be called for convenience the prepossession of a word. It is in fact the form, but there are reasons for being cautious in using form here, and it bears a valuable analogy to the soul, one however which is not complete, because all names but proper names are general while the soul is individual.

Since every definition is the definition of a word and every word may be considered as the contraction or coinciding-point of its definitions we may for convenience use word and definition with a certain freedom of interchange.

A word then has three terms belonging to it, ὅροι or moments— its prepossession of feeling; its definition, abstraction, vocal expression or other utterance; and its application, "extension," the concrete things coming under it.

It is plain that of these only one in propriety is the word; the third is not a word but a thing meant by it, the first is not a word but something connotatively meant by it, the nature of which is further to be explored.

But not even the whole field of the middle term is covered by the word. For the word is the expression, *uttering* of the idea in the mind. That idea itself has its two terms, the image (of sight or sound or *scapes* of the other senses), which is in fact physical and a refined energy[15] accenting the nerves, a word to oneself, an inchoate word, and secondly the conception.

The mind has two kinds of energy, a transitional kind, when one thought or sensation follows another, which is to reason, whether actively as in deliberation, criticism, or passively, so to call it, as in reading etc; (ii) an abiding kind for which I remember no name, in which the mind is absorbed (as far as that may be), taken up by, dwells upon, enjoys, a single thought; we may call it contemplation, but it includes pleasures, supposing they, however turbid, do not require a transition to another term *of another kind,* for contemplation in its absoluteness is impossible unless in a trance and it is enough for the mind to repeat the same energy on the same matter.

Art exacts this energy of contemplation but also the other one, and in fact they are not incompatible, for even in the successive arts as music, for full enjoyment, the synthesis of the succession should give, unlock, the contemplative enjoyment of the unity of the whole. It is however true that in the successive arts with their greater complexity and length the whole's unity retires, is less important, serves rather for the framework of that of the parts.

The more intellectual, less physical, the spell of contemplation the more complex must be the object, the more close and elaborate must be the comparison the mind has to keep making between the whole and the parts, the parts and the whole. For this reference or comparison is what the sense of unity means; mere sense that such a thing is one and not two has no interest or value except accidentally.

Works of art of course like words utter the idea and in representing real things convey the prepossession with more or less success.

---

[15]That is when deliberately formed or when a thought is recalled, for when produced by sensation from without or when as in dreams etc it presents itself unbidden it comes from the involuntary working of nature. [Hopkins's note.]

The further in anything, as a work of art, the organization is carried out, the deeper the form penetrates, the prepossession flushes the matter, the more effort will be required in apprehension, the more power of comparison, the more capacity for receiving that synthesis of (either successive or spatially distinct) impressions which gives us the unity with the prepossession conveyed by it.

The saner moreover is the act of contemplation as contemplating that which really is expressed in the object.

But some minds prefer that the prepossession they are to receive should be conveyed by the least organic, expressive, by the most suggestive, way. By this means the prepossession and the definition, uttering, are distinguished and unwound, which is the less sane attitude.

Alone with this preference for the disengaged and unconditioned prepossession in these minds is often found an intellectual attraction for very sharp and pure dialectic or, in other matter, hard and telling art-forms; in fact we have in them the two axes on which rhetoric turns.

AUTHOR'S PREFACE [16]
[c. 1883]

The poems in this book are written some in Running Rhythm, the common rhythm in English use, some in Sprung Rhythm, and some in a mixture of the two. And those in the common rhythm are some counterpointed, some not.

Common English rhythm, called Running Rhythm above, is measured by feet of either two or three syllables and (putting aside the imperfect feet at the beginning and end of lines and also some

---

[16]I.e., to the manuscript book of poems kept by his friend Robert Bridges.

unusual measures, in which feet seem to be paired together and double or composite feet to arise) never more or less.

Every foot has one principal stress or accent, and this or the syllable it falls on may be called the Stress of the foot and the other part, the one or two unaccented syllables, the Slack. Feet (and the rhythms made out of them) in which the stress comes first are called Falling Feet and Falling Rhythms, feet and rhythm in which the slack comes first are called Rising Feet and Rhythms, and if the stress is between two slacks there will be Rocking Feet and Rhythms. These distinctions are real and true to nature; but for purposes of scanning it is a great convenience to follow the example of music and take the stress always first, as the accent or the chief accent always comes first in a musical bar. If this is done there will be in common English verse only two possible feet—the so-called accentual Trochee and Dactyl, and correspondingly only two possible uniform rhythms, the so-called Trochaic and Dactylic. But they may be mixed and then what the Greeks called a Logaoedic Rhythm arises. These are the facts and according to these the scanning of ordinary regularly-written English verse is very simple indeed and to bring in other principles is here unnecessary.

But because verse written strictly in these feet and by these principles will become same and tame the poets have brought in licences and departures from rule to give variety, and especially when the natural rhythm is rising, as in the common ten-syllable or five-foot verse, rhymed or blank. These irregularities are chiefly Reversed Feet and Reversed or Counterpoint Rhythm, which two things are two steps or degrees of licence in the same kind. By a reversed foot I mean the putting the stress where, to judge by the rest of the measure, the slack should be and the slack where the stress, and this is done freely at the beginning of a line and, in the course of a line, after a pause; only scarcely ever in the second foot or place and never in the last, unless when the poet designs some extraordinary effect; for these places are characteristic and sensitive and cannot well be touched. But the reversal of the first foot and of some middle foot after a strong pause is a thing so natural that our poets have generally done it, from Chaucer down, without remark and it commonly passes unnoticed and cannot be said to amount to a formal change of rhythm, but rather is that irregularity which all natural growth and motion shews. If however the reversal is repeated in two feet running, especially so as to include the sensitive second foot, it must be due either to great want of ear or else is a calculated effect, the super-inducing or *mounting* of a new rhythm upon the old; and since the new or mounted rhythm is actually heard and at the same time the mind naturally supplies the natural standard foregoing rhythm, for we do not forget what the rhythm is that by rights we should be hearing, two rhythms are in some manner running at once and we have something answerable to counterpoint in music, which is two or more strains of tune going on together, and this is Counterpoint Rhythm. Of this kind of verse Milton is the great master and the choruses of *Samson Agonistes* are written throughout in it—but with the disadvantage that he does not let the reader clearly know what the ground-rhythm is meant to be and so they have struck most readers as merely irregular. And in fact if you counterpoint throughout, since only one of the counter rhythms is actually heard, the other is really destroyed or cannot come to exist, and what is written is one rhythm only and probably Sprung Rhythm, of which I now speak.

Sprung Rhythm, as used in this book, is measured by feet of from one to four syllables, regularly, and for particular effects any number of weak or slack syllables may be used. It has one stress, which falls on the only syllable, if there is only one, or, if there are more, then scanning as above, on the first, and so gives rise to four sorts of feet, a monosyllable and the so-called accentual Trochee, Dactyl, and the First Paeon. And there will be four corresponding natural rhythms; but nominally the feet are mixed and any one may follow any other.

And hence Sprung Rhythm differs from Running Rhythm in having or being only one nominal rhythm, a mixed of "logaoedic" one, instead of three, but on the other hand in having twice the flexibility of foot, so that any two stresses may either follow one another running or be divided by one, two, or three slack syllables. But strict Sprung Rhythm cannot be counterpointed. In Sprung Rhythm, as in logaoedic rhythm generally, the feet are assumed to be equally long or strong and their seeming inequality is made up by pause or stressing.

Remark also that it is natural in Sprung Rhythm for the lines to be *rove over,* that is for the scanning of each line immediately to take up that of the one before, so that if the first has one or more syllables at its end the other must have so many less at its beginning; and in fact the scanning runs on without a break from the beginning, say, of a stanza to the end and all the stanza is one long strain, though written in lines asunder.

Two licences are natural to Sprung Rhythm. The one is rests, as in music; but of this an example is scarcely to be found in this book, unless in the *Echos,* second line. The other is *hangers* or *outrides,* that is one, two, or three slack syllables added to a foot and not counting in the nominal scanning. They are so called because they seem to hang below the line or ride forward or backward from it in another dimension than the line itself, according to a principle needless to explain here. These outriding half feet or hangers are marked by a loop underneath them, and plenty of them will be found.

The other marks are easily understood, namely accents, where the reader might be in doubt which syllable should have the stress; slurs, that is loops *over* syllables, to tie them together into the time of one; little loops at the end of a line to shew that the rhyme goes on to the first letter of the next line; what in music are called pauses ⌒, to shew that the syllable should be dwelt on; and twirls ~, to mark reversed or counterpointed rhythm.

Note on the nature and history of Sprung Rhythm—Sprung Rhythm is the most natural of things. For (1) it is the rhythm of common speech and of written prose, when rhythm is perceived in them. (2) It is the rhythm of all but the most monotonously regular music, so that in the words of choruses and refrains and in songs written closely to music it arises. (3) It is found in nursery rhymes, weather saws, and so on; because, however these may have been once made in running rhythm, the terminations having dropped off by the change of language, the stresses come together and so the rhythm is sprung. (4) It arises in common verse when reversed or counterpointed, for the same reason.

But nevertheless in spite of all this and though Greek and Latin lyric verse, which is well known, and the old English verse seen in "Pierce [i.e., Piers] Ploughman" are in sprung rhythm, it has in fact ceased to be used since the Elizabethan age, Greene being the last writer who can be said to have recognised it. For perhaps there was not, down to our days, a single, even short, poem in English in which sprung rhythm is employed—not for single effects or in fixed places—but as the governing principle of the scansion. I say this because the contrary has been asserted: if it is otherwise the poem should be cited.

Some of the sonnets in this book are in five-foot, some in six-foot or Alexandrine lines.

["Pied Beauty" and "Peace"] are Curtal-Sonnets, that is they are constructed in proportions resembling those of the sonnet proper, namely, $6+4$ instead of $8+6$, with however a half-line tailpiece (so that the equation is rather $\frac{12}{2}+\frac{9}{2}=\frac{21}{2}=10\frac{1}{2}$).

Sermons

If we learn no more from a Gospel or a sermon on the Gospel than to know our Lord Jesus Christ better, to be prouder of him, and to love him more we learn enough and we learn a precious lesson. He is the king to whom we are to be loyal and he is the general we are to obey. The man that says to himself as he walks: Christ is my king, Christ is my hero, I am at Christ's orders, I am his to command /, that man is a child of light—*qui sequitur me non ambulat in tenebris, sed habebit lumen vitae,* who follows etc. So that it would be a good practice if you are walking alone sometimes to say over many times to yourselves: Christ is my master; then after a time: Lord, what wilt thou have me do? then to answer yourselves: My daily duties, just the duties of my station / and: I wish to do my daily duties to thy glory, my God / and in particular you may name one or more. This is mental prayer.

After saying this need only point out how our Lord behaved in the case before us. *He behaved with gentleness and secrecy* according to his wisdom; at other times according to the same wisdom with sternness and open vehemence, but here with gentleness and secrecy.

They bring him *a deaf and dumb man to be cured.* We learn from St. Matthew that *he had a devil.* That is / his deafness and etc were not natural nor due to faults of the organs, an evil spirit had possessed himself of them; a sullen stubborn spirit, hiding both himself and his victim's reason. Therefore not generally known that he was possessed, this dreadful circumstance could be concealed and the evangelist conceals it because Christ did so. It is true we learn it from

St Matthew, but after a time all reason for concealment passed away, the people could no longer be identified. To conceal then this painful circumstance our Lord took the sufferer aside. Here you see his considerateness for his creatures' feelings.

He puts his fingers into the man's ears—as if to break down the hindrance which barred up his hearing and deafened him; but gently, with the fingertips, as if it were some delicate operation the heavenly physician had in hand, not a work of mighty power. Those things which are said to be done by the Lord's arm are God's works of power, those by his finger are the subtle workings of his wisdom. Here we may understand how men through sin had become deaf to God's calls, when his son, coming in flesh, by his gentle dealings with them once more opened their hearts.

He touched his tongue with spittle from his mouth. When the mouth is parched and dry it is hard to speak, moistening it gives it the power of speech again. Here we may understand how men had ceased to pray, or to pray as they should (for the Greek says μογιλάλον, that spoke with an impediment, could hardly speak) when Christ by the sweetness of the lessons of his mouth made their tongues free and lissome again

Then having made the organs ready to hear and speak *he looked up to heaven and groaned*—It was an appeal, a prayer to his heavenly Father, full of pity for this poor possessed man and for all mankind. *And said: Ephphetha, Be opened*—The evangelist tells us the very word which had this magical or rather miraculous effect. He spoke to the man and not rebuked the devil, but the devil nevertheless fled away. *And immediately etc*

Then our Lord told the cured patient and his friends *not to speak of it,* but the ears he had opened did not heed him nor the tongue he had loosened obey. Nevertheless little harm, as I suppose, was done by this: for their own interest he had kept the matter quiet and bidden them do so; but, if they chose to speak, their interests and their good name were now in their own keeping to do as they liked with. Besides he would not punish them for preferring his honour to their own

He hath done all things well etc—that is / the whole thing. They admired the completeness and delicacy of the cure. Much more should we admire what Christ has done for us—made us deaf hear, if we will hear, not with a touch of his fingertips but with his hands hardnailed out and appealingly stretched on the cross; made us dumb speak in praise and prayer to God not by a moistening of spittle but by the shedding of all his precious blood

FOR SUNDAY NOV. 9 1879,
ST. JOSEPH'S, BEDFORD LEIGH —
on the Healing of Jairus' Daughter and the Woman with the Issue of Blood
(Gospel Matt. 9:18–26: see Mark 5:22 sqq., Luke 8:41 sqq.)

In this Gospel *two miracles, not one after the other, but* first the beginning of one, then the other, then the end of the first; as when you drive a quill or straw or knitting needle *through an egg,* it pierces first the white, then the yolk, then the white again. And in the two other accounts the same, though commonly the Evangelists change the order of things freely according to the purpose they have in hand; but here they all agree to follow the order of the events. There must be a reason for this and there is.

We read of many miracles our Lord worked. There were no doubt many more we do not read of, but whatever the number of the whole *there might of course have been more,* many more; all the sick in the world were not cured, not all in the Holy Land nor all even in Jerusalem. He cured then many but he might have cured far more.

And then there are all those that lived before his coming and that have lived since. *Miseratio hominis circa proximum suum, misericordia autem Domini super omnia opera sua* / a man shews mercy upon his neighbour, but the Lord's mercy is over all his works: our Lord came as man; as God he pitied all, but as man he cured only his neighbours in place and time, and not all of them, but some he cured and some he did not. He acted according to providence and prudence, he acted on a plan, and his plan took in some and left out others. He looked first to the soul to cure that, the cure of the body was always to help towards the cure of the soul, and where it would not help no doubt the miracle was not wrought; again he looked to the general good, the good of the one was to help towards the good of the many, and where it would not help the miracle was either not wrought or was not wrought in public. And in general you will find that what Christ aimed at in his miracles was to breed faith in him or it being bred to nurse it; to breed it and to nurse it, I say, both in the receiver of the miracle and in all who should witness it or hear of it. You will please, brethren, take notice of this with me in the two miracles of today's Gospel. Not only so but in these two miracles he was teaching lessons, besides faith, of hope and of brotherly charity.

There came to him then *a ruler* and, as we read elsewhere, a ruler of the synagogue. Such men were not, we know, friendly to him, they were his bitterest enemies. And this man, Jaïrus himself, he perhaps, had things gone prosperously with him, for prosperity feeds pride, might never have come to Christ; but love will drive men to shifts, *sorrow bows the proud head;* his daughter, his only child, in her first-bloom had drooped, lay dying; she had been given over, hope was out, and yet it was not the father saw one hope, the prophet of Nazareth, to him he made his way. He did his pride down to the ground, he sent no messengers, he made no measured and reserved advances, upon his knees he fell, he ended low, and with earnest and humble entreaties from a broken heart he besought help for his dying daughter.

My daughter, we read he said, *is even now dead.* Another account tells us he said she was *dying.* How is this? You may say, if you like that he *meant* she was dying but to shew how near to death she was, how extreme her need, how great his own anguish he called her dead; so that one way of telling the story would shew us what his meaning was, the other what his very words were. This may be, *this is a good explanation, but there is a better,* which will come in its place presently. Meantime I shall suppose / what he really said was that his daughter was dying.

But come, lay thy hand upon her and she shall live. Here you see what *his faith was, true but shortsighted.* Christ must come, must touch the child; if he but touched her he was sure she would live, but his power, he seemed to think, did not reach beyond his fingertips; eager, in all haste as the man was / it did not occur to him to shorten the road and make a way through the crowd by a miracle worked there and then; no but Christ must rise and come; accordingly Christ, as his manner was, took him at his word, arose, and went.

We read in St. Mark that *a great crowd followed and thronged him.* Take notice of this. If there ever was a time when a man could have wished the road clear and no bar or hindrance in the way it was then. And the crowds must needs follow and throng him! Fancy, my brethren, fancy that father: the crowd was between Christ and his daughter's life. They, those lusty men and women, for no doubt they seemed strong and hale enough, with all their sound limbs thrusting and thronging were crushing out the last spark of life from one poor girl's spent and wasted body. They were, for they would not make way fast enough for Christ to come at her. Alas, and this was not enough. At this most unhappy, most unseasonable, most agonising moment, comes in that woman with the issue of blood, she that could have come and better come at any time but that, and there must be a delay and a search for her made and an opening cleared and questions asked and a discourse delivered and his daughter every precious moment dying or perhaps dead. Indeed he was right; what he feared we know, the worst had come, she *was* dead, and the messengers were at that moment on their way to tell him.

Now as this afflicted father had to wait while Christ healed the woman and as the Evangelists make his story wait, turning to the woman's, so let us leave him awhile and turn to her. She had been sick, we read, twelve years. Now the sick girl was twelve years old. So many years as that child had had of life so many had this woman had of sickness, to the girl they had been years of growth and gain, to the woman they had been of loss and wasting, grievous loss in purse and person. But now the girl's case was worse than hers, for her fresh life was that hour passing away and the woman's wasted one might spend and be spent for some wretched years longer. However these two were to glorify God by their cures on one and the same day.

She said within herself etc—The event shewed she was right. True, she might have been cured at a distance, but God may have inspired the thought nevertheless. Her disease might suggest it: that stained and defiled her garments and made unclean those she touched, Christ her saviour to his very garment conveyed a healing and a cleansing virtue. There need then be no want of faith in this nor selfishness in wanting to be cured first then, for she may not have known of Jairus' need or thought her cure would hinder his daughter's. But her faith came short in this, that she thought Christ would not know, and she was selfish in this, that she meant the cure to benefit none but herself and left out of sight God's glory and her neighbour's advantage: She said *within herself.*

Christ' wisdom: the same act should build up both her faith and the father's, correct both her self love and that father's.

FOR SUNDAY EVENING NOV. 23 1879
AT BEDFORD LEIGH—
Et erat pater ejus et mater mirantes super his quae dicebantur de illo
(text taken at random)
Luke 2:33.

St. Joseph though he often carried our Lord Jesus Christ in his arms and the Blessed Virgin though she gave him birth and suckled him at her breast, though they seldom either of them had the holy child out of their sight and knew more of him far than all others, yet when they heard what Holy Simeon a stranger had to say of him the Scripture says they wondered. Not indeed that they were surprised and had thought to hear something different but that they gave their minds up to admiration and dwelt with reverent wonder on all God's doings about the child their sacred charge. Brethren, see what a thing it is to hear about our Lord Jesus Christ, to think of him and dwell upon him; it did good to these two holiest people, the Blessed Virgin and St. Joseph, even with him in the house God thought fit to give them lights by the mouth of strangers. It cannot but do good to us, who have more need of holiness, who easily forget Christ, who have not got him before our eyes to look at. And though we do have him before our eyes, masked in the Sacred Host, at mass and Benediction and within our lips receive him at communion, yet to hear of him and dwell on the thought of him will do us good.

Our Lord Jesus Christ, my brethren, is our hero, a hero all the world wants. You know how books of tales are written, that put one man before the reader and shew him off handsome for the most part and brave and call him My Hero or Our Hero. Often mothers make a hero of a son; girls of a sweetheart and good wives of a husband. Soldiers make a hero of a great general, a party of its leader, a nation of any great man that brings it glory, whether king, warrior, statesman, thinker, poet, or whatever it shall be. But Christ, he is the hero.

He too is the hero of a book or books, of the divine Gospels. He is a warrior and a conqueror; of whom it is written he went forth conquering and to conquer. He is a king, Jesus of Nazareth king of the Jews, though when he came to his own kingdom his own did not receive him, and now, his people having cast him off, we Gentiles are his inheritance. He is a statesman, that drew up the New Testament in his blood and founded the Roman Catholic Church that cannot fail. He is a thinker, that taught us divine mysteries. He is an orator and poet, as in his eloquent words and parables appears. He is all the world's hero, the desire of nations. But besides he is the hero of single souls; his mother's hero, not out of motherly foolish fondness but because he was, as the angel told her, great and the son of the Most High and all that he did and said and was done and said about him she laid up in her heart. He is the true-love and the bridegroom of men's souls: the virgins follow him whithersoever he goes; the martyrs follow him through a sea of blood, through great tribulation; all his servants take up their cross and follow him. And those even that do not follow him, yet they look wistfully after him, own him a hero, and wish they dared answer to his call. Children as soon as they can understand ought to be told about him, that they may make him the hero of their young hearts. But there are Catholic parents that shamefully neglect their duty: the grown children of Catholics are found that scarcely know or do not know his name. Will such parents say they left instruction to the priest or the schoolmaster? Why, if they sent them very early to the school they might make that excuse, but when they do not what will they say then? It is at the father's or the mother's mouth first the little one should learn. But the parents may be gossipping or drinking and the children have not heard of their lord and saviour. Those of you, my brethren, who are young and yet unmarried resolve that when you marry, if God should bless you with children, this shall not be but that you will have more pity, will have pity upon your own.

There met in Jesus Christ all things that can make man lovely and loveable. In his body he was most beautiful. This is known first by the tradition in the Church that it was so and by holy writers agreeing to suit those words to him / Thou art beautiful in mould above the sons of men:[17] we have even accounts of him written in early times. They tell us that he was moderately tall, well built and tender in frame, his features straight and beautiful, his hair inclining to auburn, parted in the midst, curling and clustering about the ears and neck as the leaves of a filbert, so they speak, upon the nut. He wore also a forked beard and this as well as the locks upon his head were never touched by razor or shears; neither, his health being perfect, could a hair ever fall to the ground. The account I have been quoting (it is from memory, for I cannot now lay my hand upon it) we do not indeed for certain know to be correct, but it has been current in the Church and many generations have drawn our Lord accordingly either in their own minds or in his images. Another proof of his beauty may be drawn from the words *proficiebat sapientia et aetate et gratia apud Deum et homines* [Luke 2:52] / he went forward in wisdom and bodily frame and favour with God and men; that is / he pleased both God and men daily more and more by his growth of mind and body. But he could not have pleased by growth of body unless the body was strong, healthy, and beautiful that grew. But the best proof of all is this, that his body was the special work of the Holy Ghost. He was not born in nature's course, no man was his father; had he been born as others are he must have inherited some defect of figure or of constitution, from which no man born as fallen men are born is wholly free unless God interfere to keep him so. But his body was framed directly from heaven by the power of the Holy Ghost, of whom it would be unworthy to leave any the least botch or failing in his work. So the first Adam was moulded by God himself

[17]Ps. 44:3 (Vulgate).

[139]

and Eve built up by God too out of Adam's rib and they could not but be pieces, both, of faultless workmanship: the same then and much more must Christ have been. His constitution too was tempered perfectly, he had neither disease nor the seeds of any: weariness he felt when he was wearied, hunger when he fasted, thirst when he had long gone without drink, but to the touch of sickness he was a stranger. I leave it to you, brethren, then to picture him, in whom the fullness of the godhead dwelt bodily, in his bearing how majestic, how strong and yet how lovely and lissome in his limbs, in his look how earnest, grave but kind. In his Passion all this strength was spent, this lissomness crippled, this beauty wrecked, this majesty beaten down. But now it is more than all restored, and for myself I make no secret I look forward with eager desire to seeing the matchless beauty of Christ's body in the heavenly light.

I come to his mind. He was the greatest genius that ever lived. You know what genius is, brethren—beauty and perfection in the mind. For perfection in the bodily frame distinguishes a man among other men his fellows: so may the mind be distinguished for its beauty above other minds and that is genius. Then when this genius is duly taught and trained, that is wisdom; for without training genius is imperfect and again wisdom is imperfect without genius. But Christ, we read, advanced in wisdom and in favour with God and men: now this wisdom, in which he excelled all men, had to be founded on an unrivalled genius. Christ then was the greatest genius that ever lived. You must not say, Christ needed no such thing as genius; his wisdom came from heaven, for he was God. To say so is to speak like the heretic Apollinaris, who said that Christ had indeed a human body but no soul, he needed no mind and soul, for his godhead, the Word of God, that stood for mind and soul in him. No, but Christ was perfect man and must have mind as well as body and that mind was, no question, of the rarest excellence and beauty; it was genius. As Christ lived and breathed and moved in a true and not a phantom human body and in that laboured, suffered, was crucified, died, and was buried; as he merited by acts of his human will; so he reasoned and planned and invented by acts of his own human genius,[18] genius made perfect by wisdom of its own, not the divine wisdom only.

A witness to his genius we have in those men who being sent to arrest him came back empty handed, spellbound by his eloquence, saying / Never man spoke like this man.

A better proof we have in his own words, his sermon on the mount, his parables, and all his sayings recorded in the Gospel. My brethren, we are so accustomed to them that they do not strike us as they do a stranger that hears them first, else we too should say / Never man etc. No stories or parables are like Christ's, so bright, so pithy, so touching; no proverbs or sayings are such jewellery: they stand off from other men's thoughts like stars, like lilies in the sun; nowhere in literature is there anything to match the Sermon on the Mount: if there is let men bring it forward. Time does not allow me to call your minds to proofs or instances. Besides Christ's sayings in the Gospels a dozen or so more have been kept by tradition and are to be found in the works of the Fathers and early writers and one even in the Scripture itself: It is more blessed etc.[19] When these sayings are gathered together, though one cannot feel sure of every one, yet reading all in one view they make me say / These must be Christ's, never man etc. One is: Never rejoice but when you look upon your brother in love. Another is: My mystery is for me and for the children of my house.

And if you wish for another still greater proof of his genius and wisdom look at this Catholic Church that he founded, its ranks and constitution, its rites and sacraments.

---

[18]I.e., Christ was uniquely individual, like any other human being.
[19]Acts 20:35.

Now in the third place, far higher than beauty of the body, higher than genius and wisdom the beauty of the mind, comes the beauty of his character, his character as man. For the most part his very enemies, those that do not believe in him, allow that a character so noble was never seen in human mould. Plato the heathen, the greatest of the Greek philosophers, foretold of him: he drew by his wisdom a picture of the just man in his justice crucified and it was fulfilled in Christ. Poor was his station, laborious his life, bitter his ending: through poverty, through labour, through crucifixion his majesty of nature more shines. No heart as his was ever so tender, but tenderness was not all: this heart so tender was as brave, it could be stern. He found the thought of his Passion past bearing, yet he went through with it. He was feared when he chose: he took a whip and single-handed cleared the temple. The thought of his gentleness towards children, towards the afflicted, towards sinners, is often dwelt on; that of his courage less. But for my part I like to feel that I should have feared him. We hear also of his love, as for John and Lazarus; and even love at first sight, as of the young man that had kept all the commandments from his childhood. But he warned or rebuked his best friends when need was, as Peter, Martha, and even his mother. For, as St. John says, he was full both of grace and of truth.

But, brethren, from all that might be said of his character I single out one point and beg you to notice that. He loved to praise, he loved to reward. He knew what was in man, he best knew men's faults and yet he was the warmest in their praise. When he worked a miracle he would grace it with / Thy faith hath saved thee, that it might almost seem the receiver's work, not his. He said of Nathanael that he was an Israelite without guile; he that searches hearts said this, and yet what praise that was to give! He called the two sons of Zebedee Sons of Thunder, kind and stately and honourable name! We read of nothing thunderlike that they did except, what was sinful, to wish fire down from heaven on some sinners, but they deserved the name or he would not have given it, and he has given it them for all time. Of John the Baptist he said that his greater was not born of women. He said to Peter / Thou art Rock / and rewarded a moment's acknowledgement of him with the lasting leadership of his Church. He defended Magdalen and took means that the story of her generosity should be told for ever. And though he bids *us* say we are unprofitable servants, yet he himself will say to each of us / Good and faithful servant, well done.

And this man whose picture I have tried to draw for you, brethren, is your God. He was your maker in time past; hereafter he will be your judge. Make him your hero now. Take some time to think of him; praise him in your hearts. You can over your work or on your road praise him, saying over and over again / Glory be to Christ's body; Glory to the body of the Word made flesh; Glory to the body suckled at the Blessed Virgin's breasts; Glory to Christ's body in its beauty; Glory to Christ's body in its weariness; Glory to Christ's body in its Passion, death and burial; Glory to Christ's body risen; Glory to Christ's body in the Blessed Sacrament; Glory to Christ's soul; Glory to his genius and wisdom; Glory to his unsearchable thoughts; Glory to his saving words; Glory to his sacred heart; Glory to its courage and manliness; Glory to its meekness and mercy; Glory to its every heartbeat, to its joys and sorrows, wishes, fears; Glory in all things to Jesus Christ God and man. If you try this when you can you will find your heart kindle and while you praise him he will praise you—a blessing etc

A. M. D. G.

FOR SUNDAY EVENING DEC. 14 1879,

3RD IN ADVENT, AT ST. JOSEPH'S BEDFORD —

on *Gaudete in Domino semper: iterum dico, gaudete. Modestia vestra nota sit omnibus hominibus. Dominus prope est*—

Phil. 4:4, 5. (from the Epistle)

Since *we have a procession tonight* I wish, brethren, to be but short. "Rejoice in the Lord always," says the Apostle; "again I say, rejoice": we do rejoice, we have a procession, which is a joyous and festival thing, and in the Lord, for it is in his honour and his Blessed Mother's. However the procession will not last long, tonight is not always, and we are always, he says, to rejoice in the Lord. I will speak then of this always rejoicing in the Lord.

If we are *to rejoice in the Lord we must be in his grace,* we must be out of mortal sin. How can a mortal sinner rejoice in the Lord? He has offended the Lord, the Lord is his judge, the Lord condemns him, what joy can he have to think of him? Nay what joy at all? since he is under sentence, is threatened with hell, everlasting fire is his portion; how can he forget that dreadful thought? how can he have any joy at all?—but he can; I will not deny they do; they drown thought in drink and passing pleasure; it is not happiness, but enjoyment of a sort it is, and yet life is full of deaths and dangers, many above ground and underground more still. But if the man has faith and fears, though he does not serve God, what is this joy worth? He hears of a sudden death and he is touched with fear, fear poisons pleasure, it embitters his sweet cup and stings him in his easy bed. And far better it should, since it may bring him to repentance, than that he should live at ease and dying wake in hell. There is a crowd of you, brethren, and amidst that crowd some must be in this road— I mean are out of your duty, out of God's grace, and in mortal sin. You are cowardly, you are slothful, and with that you are insolent:

you are bold to break God's law and yet you are not bold enough to help your own souls. [Here add a few words.][20]

Rejoice in the Lord is said to those who love God, whose sins are forgiven, for whom a crown is laid up in heaven. This is a joy which nothing, which no man, as our Lord said to his Apostles, can take from you. Otherwise there are many who could not rejoice. One might say: I am in such want that I am not sure of my next meal: how can I have any joy? Another says: I have just lost a child, a wife or a husband: how can I rejoice? Another is in sickness or pain or ill-used or slandered by unkind tongues. The things I have named are afflictions, they are sorrows so great that for a time they may take from the world all comfort, but they leave you your heavenly hope; of that comfort they cannot rob you. If you are poor, why then you are blessed because yours is the kingdom of heaven; if meek, that is patiently bearing illtreatment, you are blessed because you are to inherit the earth; if a mourner you are blessed because you are to be comforted; and so forth. If you say that when all is said you feel your sorrows still; why yes, for comfort is not to undo what is done and yet it is comfort, yet it comforts. If we feel the comfort little, there, my brethren, is our fault and want of faith; we must put a stress on ourselves and make ourselves find comfort where we know the comfort is to be found. It *is* a comfort that in spite of all, God loves us; it *is* a comfort that the sufferings of this present world (St. Paul says) are not worthy to be compared with the glory that is to be revealed in us; such thoughts *are* comfort, we have only to force ourselves to see it, to dwell on it, and at last to feel that it is so. Cheerfulness has ever been a mark of saints and good people. The Apostles went rejoicing we read, after their scourging from the sight of the Council, because they were found worthy for the name of Jesus to suffer insult; the martyrs were cheerful: when at one time the Christians were led to

[20]Hopkins's brackets (Eds.)

execution mingled, through their persecutors' malice, with common convicts / all would not do, the martyrs by their joyous looks could easily be told from those who were to suffer the just reward of their crimes; Margaret Clitheroe[21] as she went through York streets, to be pressed to death on Ouse Bridge, all along the road as best she could with her pinioned hands dealing out alms to the poor, looked, it is said, so marvellously cheerful and happy that her murderers, like those Pharisees who of Christ her master said that he cast out devils by Beelzebub, had nothing for it but to pretend she was possessed by "a merry devil." Goodness then, my brethren, is cheerful and no wonder, and if there are, as to be sure there are, some good people whose looks are commonly downcast and sad, that is a fault in them and they are not to be copied in it.

I have been speaking of a holy joy which those who are in God's grace may have even in the midst of their sorrows and misfortunes, but most people at most times are not, most of you now are not, in sorrow and misfortune: henceforward I am going to speak for the most part of people, for the most part of you, how you should rejoice in the Lord—always understood that you are in God's grace and free from sin. "Rejoice in the Lord always; again I say, rejoice"—and how?—The secret is soon out: *by dearly loving the Lord himself, our Lord Jesus Christ.* If this world is going fairly well with you you have no such need, just for the time, to long for another, better one: you should of course always hope for it, but you are not forced to do so as a relief and comfort against the trials of this. But to rejoice in the thought of our Lord Jesus Christ, that we should always do, not only to sweeten our sorrows but also to sanctify our joys.

(The rest shorter)—Love of God means the preferring his will to ours: it is the love of a subject for his ruler. By this we shall be saved,

---

[21]A Catholic martyred in 1586 for sheltering priests. Hopkins's poem on her death (untitled) was probably written in 1876 or 1877.

but this is but a cold sort of love. Love for Christ is enthusiasm for a leader, a hero, love for a bosom friend, love for a lover. Now when we love God he first loved us, first loved us as a ruler his subjects before we loved him as subjects their ruler; so when we love Christ with a fonder love than that / he with a fonder love than that first loved us. It has been said that God prays to men more than men to God: Christ called to us from his cross more than we call to him there. We call to him for comfort, but long ago he said: Come unto me. Long before John or Edward, Margaret or Elisabeth ever said / I love our Lord Jesus Christ / he said / I love John, I love Edward, I love Margaret, I love Elisabeth. His servants rejoice in him, at least St. Paul says they should, but much more does Christ rejoice in them. Are they handsome, healthy, strong, ableminded, witty, successful, brave, truthful, pure, just? He admires them more than they can, more than they *justly* can, themselves, for he made all these things, beauty, health, strength, and the rest. But we admire ourselves and pride ourselves: we should leave that to him, he is proud enough of us. If we do well he smiles, he claps his hands over us; he is interested in our undertakings, he does not always grant them success, but he is more interested in them than we are. The wife wants her master a good husband, Christ wants it more; the child wishes him a good father, Christ etc; the employer wants him a faithful workman, he is satisfied with moderately good work, Christ is not, he looks at it with a keener artist's eye; and so on. We must then take an interest in Christ, because he first took an interest in us; *rejoice in him because he has first rejoiced in us.*

FOR SUNDAY APRIL 25TH [1880], THE 4TH AFTER
EASTER, AT ST. FRANCIS XAVIER'S, LIVERPOOL,
on the Gospel John 16:5–14. and in particular 8–11
(*"arguet mundum de peccato et de justitia et de judicio,"* etc.)

Notes (for it seems that written sermons do no good)—This Gospel
and those for the other Sundays after Easter taken from Christ's dis-
courses *before* Easter, before his Passion, and in particular from the
discourse delivered at the Last Supper. They are out of their season
and why. Cannot give them the proper attention when engrossed
with the Passion. But when he should be done, Christ said, the Holy
Ghost would remind them of what he had said: that time is now
and, very suitably, at the earliest opportunity after Easter.

(However the Rector wishes me to write)

Brethren, you see that this Gospel I have just read is taken from
that discourse which Christ our Lord made to his disciples the night
before he suffered. So is the Gospel for last Sunday, so is the Gospel
for next Sunday. The words we read in these Gospels were spoken
before Easter, on the night before the Passion, and we read them *after*
Easter. They come then out of their season. But this cannot be
helped; it is reasonable, it is wise and right. During Lent, during
Passiontide, it is the Church's wish that the minds of Christians
should be full of the Passion, should be engrossed with Christ's suf-
ferings: the mind cannot pay full and proper heed to two thoughts at
once, cannot be in two moods at once, and so it cannot, if it is fixed on
Christ's sorrows and what he underwent, be free to dwell on Christ's
wisdom and the words he said. That must be put off, it has been
wisely put off till after Easter and yet not long after, but at the first
suitable opportunity to Christ's words the Church returns and so
you hear them in last Sunday's and today's and next Sunday's
Gospels. But indeed Christ's own words on that same occasion
explain all: This, he says (14:26), I have said to you while with you,

but when the Holy Ghost is come, *he* will teach you all my meaning and remind you of all I have said. That time is now come: Christ is gone to heaven, the Holy Ghost has been sent and is, and has long been, at his work of teaching the Church Christ's meaning and reminding it of Christ's words. Therefore it comes about that with the assistance of the same Holy Ghost I must this morning endeavour to bring out Christ's meaning in that Gospel which is this day appointed to be read.

[Begin thus—] In the Gospel which you have just heard, brethren, are words reckoned etc

And that, brethren, is no easy task; for in this same Gospel of today are found words reckoned by writers on Holy Scripture to be among the very darkest and most mysterious that the sacred page contains. But since many enlightened minds and many learned pens have in the course of Catholic ages been busied upon them, it is now to be supposed that this darkness and mystery is in part cleared up and that with their help we need not go far astray. Bend then, my brethren, your ears and minds to follow and understand, for it is the Church that has appointed the words to be read and not for nothing, not for us to stare or sleep over them but to heed them and take their meaning; besides that it seems to me a contemptible and unmanly thing, for men whose minds are naturally clear, to give up at the first hearing of a hard passage in the Scripture and in the holiest of all kinds of learning to care to know no more than children know.

Here then are the mysterious words which we are to consider: *And when he,* that is the Holy Ghost, whom our Lord in this place calls the Paraclete, *has come he will convince the world of sin and of justice and of judgment,* and he adds a reason to each: *of sin,* he says, *because* so and so, *of justice because* so and so, *and of judgment because* so and so. This is what needs explanation and in explaining it / by these steps I shall go: first I shall say what a Paraclete is and how both Christ and the Holy Ghost are Paracletes; then I shall shew what a

Paraclete has to do with those three things, sin and justice and judgment; lastly I shall shew why Christ as a Paraclete would not do alone, why it was better for him to go and another Paraclete to come, why Christ's struggle with the world taken by itself looked like a failure when the Holy Ghost's struggling with the world is a success. And in so speaking the meaning of the text will, I hope, have by degrees grown plain.

The first is to say what a Paraclete means. As when the Holy Ghost came on Whitsunday upon the Apostles there was heard a rush of air before the tongues of fire were seen / so when we hear this name of Paraclete our ears and minds are filled with a confused murmuring of some mystery which we know to have to do with the Holy Ghost. For God the Holy Ghost is the Paraclete, but what is a Paraclete? often it is translated Comforter, but a Paraclete does more than comfort. The word is Greek; there is no one English word for it and no one Latin word, *Comforter* is not enough. A Paraclete is one who comforts, who cheers, who encourages, who persuades, who exhorts, who stirs up, who urges forward, who calls on; what the spur and word of command is to a horse, what clapping of hands is to a speaker, what a trumpet is to the soldier, that a Paraclete is to the soul: *one who calls us on,* that is what it means, a Paraclete is one who calls us on to good. One sight is before my mind, it is homely but it comes home: you have seen at cricket how when one of the batsmen at the wicket has made a hit and wants to score a run, the other doubts, hangs back, or is ready to run in again, how eagerly the first will cry / Come on, come on!—a Paraclete is just that, something that cheers the spirit of man, with signals and with cries, all zealous that he should do something and full of assurance that if he will he can, calling him on, springing to meet him half way, crying to his ears or to his heart: This way to do God's will, this way to save your soul, come on, come on!

If this is to be a Paraclete, one who cries to the heart / Come on, no wonder Christ is a Paraclete. For he was one, he said so himself; though the Holy Ghost bears the name, yet Christ is a Paraclete too: *I will send you,* he says, *another Paraclete,* meaning that he himself was a Paraclete, the first Paraclete, the Holy Ghost the second. And did he not cry men on? Not only by words, as by his marvellous teaching and preaching; not only by standards and signals, as by his splendid miracles; but best of all by deeds, by his own example: he led the way, went before his troops, was himself the vanguard, was the forlorn hope, bore the brunt of battle alone, died upon the field, on Calvary hill, and bought the victory by his blood. He cried men on; he said to his disciples, Peter and Andrew, James and John, Matthew at the custom-house, and the rest: Follow me; they did so; he warned all: He that would come after me let him deny himself and take up his cross and follow me; but when they would not follow he let them go and took the war upon himself. *I have told you,* he said to those who came to arrest him, *that I am Jesus of Nazareth: if therefore you seek me let these go their way.* For though Christ cheered them on they feared to follow, though the Captain led the way the soldiers fell back; he was not for that time a successful Paraclete: *all,* it says, *they all forsook him and fled.* Not that they wanted will; *the spirit was willing: Let us go too,* said Thomas, *that we may die with him;* Peter was ready to follow him to prison and to death; *but the flesh was weak:* Peter denied him in his Passion, Thomas in his resurrection, and all of them, *all forsook him and fled.* I say these things, brethren, to shew you that God himself may be the Paraclete, God himself may cheer men on and they too be willing to follow and yet *not* follow, not come on; something may still be wanting; and therefore Christ said: *It is for your own good that I should go; for if I do not go away the Paraclete will not come to you, whereas if I go I shall send him to you.* The second Paraclete was to do what the first did not, he was to cheer men on *and they to follow;* therefore he is called, and Christ is not called, *the* Paraclete.

(2) I have said, brethren, what a Paraclete is and shewn that God the Son as well as God the Holy Ghost is a Paraclete. Next I am to say *what a Paraclete has to do with those three things—sin and justice and judgment.*

If a Paraclete is one who cheers us on to good it must be good that is hard, good that left to ourselves we should hardly reach or not reach at all; it must be in the face of hardships, difficulties, resistance, enemies, that he cheers us on. For now, after the Fall, good in this world is hard, it is surrounded by difficulties, the way to it lies through thorns, the flesh is against it, the world is against it, the Devil is against it: therefore if a Paraclete cheers men on it will be to good that is hard. Now one way or another all that makes good hard is / or comes from / sin. So that a Paraclete must cheer us on to good *in the face of sin.* And one question out of three is soon answered: we see well enough what a Paraclete has to do with sin.

But a Paraclete has also to do with justice. And how?—Why, justice is that very good to which the Paraclete cheers men on. Justice in the Scripture means goodness. If a Paraclete cheers men on to goodness / that is to say he cheers them on to justice. ["And yet" etc—omit all down to the end of the paragraph][22] And yet, mark you, cheering men on against sin is not the same as cheering men on to justice, though now the two things go together. For if there were no sin in the world and yet man as dull in mind and heart as he is now / a Paraclete might well be needed still to stir him up and set him on, to shew him what justice was and how great its beauty, before man would rouse himself to pursue it. And again if there were no true goodness in the world, nothing, I mean, that would make men just before God, yet if his law still bound them, forbidding sin, they would need a Paraclete to cheer them in resisting sin. However now the Paraclete does both at once, cheers us on to follow justice and to

[22]Hopkins's brackets (Eds.)

stand against sin. So much then of what a Paraclete has to do with sin and with justice.

There remains what a Paraclete has to do with judgment. Though the Paraclete's voice cry to men to come on to justice and cry to them to stand firm against sin, this will not do alone; the bare word will not do, nay the bare example will not do; there must be some bait before them and some spur or sting behind. This bait and this spur are the thought of God's judgments. There is the bait or prize of hope, the crown in heaven for the just, and there is the spur of fear, the fire of hell for the sinner. And the Paraclete waves before them that golden prize and plies their hearts with that smarting spur. And thus, brethren, it is clearly brought out that a Paraclete has to do, has everything to do, with sin, with justice, and with judgment.

(3) And now lastly we are to hear why it was good that Christ the first Paraclete should go and the Holy Ghost the second Paraclete, *the* Paraclete, should come and why this second Paraclete was to accomplish that task in the world which the first had not, *in his lifetime,* succeeded in accomplishing. This task was to convince the world of sin, of justice, and of judgment. The reason why Christ did not and the Holy Ghost does is not certainly that God the Son is less powerful than God the Holy Ghost: *the Father,* says the Athanasian Creed, *is almighty, the Son almighty, the Holy Ghost almighty, and they are not three almighties, but one almighty;* their almightiness, their might, their power is one and the same thing. Neither is the reason that though Christ as God is almighty as man he is weak. No, *for the Father,* we read, *had put all things into his hands.* To understand it let us look at what this convincing the world of sin, justice, and judgment means.

When then it is said that the Paraclete *will convince the world* of three things it is meant that he will convict the world of its being wrong about these things, will convince it of himself being right about them, will take it to task about them, reprove it, and so bring the force and truth of his reproof home to it as to leave it no answer to make. He will take it to task upon three heads and leave it no answer. Now did Christ do this, did he leave the world no answer?—Certainly not. To all that Christ taught and did the world's answer was to put him to death and when he rose from the dead the world's answer for a time was that his disciples had stolen his corpse away—for a time; that is to say / till the Holy Ghost came.

The world to which Christ spoke was, you know, not the world at large, not the Roman empire, much less the other kingdoms of the earth; he spoke only, as he said himself, to the House of Israel. And he did not convince the world he spoke to, he did not convince Israel. Neither indeed has the Holy Ghost convinced them yet, but then they are not the world he speaks to; they are but a very little part of it. To Christ they were the only world he spoke to and he did not convince them of his being in the right, did not convict them of their being in the wrong, on sin or on justice or on judgment. He spoke to them first of sin: he sent the Baptist before him to preach the baptism of repentance, then he came himself saying, as we read (Matt. 4:17.): *Repent, for the kingdom of heaven is at hand.* Did they repent? remember that when we say the world we mean most people, not a few: did most of the Jews, did the world of them repent?—They added to their sins by unbelief, they crowned their unbelief by crucifying him, the very prophet and Paraclete that thus reproved them.

Again he spoke to them of justice. He preached the Sermon on the Mount; he set before the world of them a new standard of goodness and of holiness; a justice higher than that, he said, of their Scribes and Pharisees; a justice indeed without which he said they could not enter into the kingdom of heaven, could not be saved. And not by words only but by his own example; he *did* and taught, he went about doing good, he challenged them himself to prove a fault against him: *Which of you,* he asked, *convinces* or *convicts me of sin?* They could not prove but they could accuse, they could not convict and yet they would condemn: they called him glutton and winebibber, sabbathbreaker, false prophet, blasphemer, deserving of death, no matter by what name, *a malefactor* any road, crying without shame to the Roman governor when he asked for a particular change: *If he were not a* MALEFACTOR *we would not have brought him to thee.* And they prevailed: as a malefactor he was judged, between thieves he was crucified, *cum iniquis reputatus est* / he was counted among evildoers, Jesus Christ the just. So they were not convicted about sin nor about justice, they were not left without an answer, Crucify him / was their answer, and they crucified him.

Of judgment it is the same. He warned them of God's judgments: unless they repented, he said, they should all perish; unless they believed in him they should die in their sins; the fallen angel was their father, his desires they would do and of course would share his fall; Depart, they would hear said of them, cursed, into everlasting fire, prepared for the Devil and his angels. Their answer was still the same: *he* was the sinner, the blasphemer, and cursed by God; it was *he* that was on the Devil's side and cast out devils by Beelzebub prince of the devils; it was *he* that by God's own law deserved to die—and should die too, by stoning or somehow: they failed to stone him, get him crucified they did. The world was not convinced about judgment nor put to silence; *he* was put to silence, put to trial, put to death, got rid of. And, mark you, brethren, it was not like a martyrdom now: the tyrant when he has done his worst upon the martyr knows that he has but cut off one Christian or ten or a thousand, there are others yet that he cannot reach; he may wreak his rage on Christians, he cannot rid the world of Christianity. But when Christ the shepherd was struck down the sheep were scattered and without him would not have reunited; when the head was off the body would go to pieces; when Christ died all his words and works came to the ground, all seemed over for ever and the world his enemy's triumph looked that day complete.

But they did not know that their seeming triumph was total defeat, that his seeming defeat was glorious victory. For it was not the world Christ had come to fight but the ruler of this world the Devil. The world he came not to condemn but to save: *God did not send his son into the world,* Christ said, *to judge* (or *condemn*) *the world but that by him the world might be saved.* Only while he preached to them, trying to save them, they were judged by their way of receiving him; therefore he said *Now it is the trial of the world, now the ruler of the world is to be cast out; and I, though taken off the earth, got rid of from the earth, shall draw all things to me.* This then had happened: the rulers of this world, the devils, had crucified the Lord of Glory and at the instant of his death they saw themselves defeated, condemned, cast out, their empire of sin over the souls of men undone and the reins of power on all things drawn into the hand of the crucified victim. They felt it with unutterable dismay and despair but the world did not at that time feel it; the hellish head was crushed but the earthly members were not aware of a wound. They were therefore not convinced or convicted of their sin, of Christ's justice, or of God's judgments.

Christ was gone and in 50 days the Holy Ghost the new Paraclete came. He lost no time, but from nine o'clock in the morning of the first Whitsunday began his untiring age-long ever conquering task of convincing the world about sin and justice and judgment. But first he would play the Paraclete among the disciples before he went out to convince and convert the world. First he cheered *them,* but he cheered them on not like Christ by his example from without but by his presence, his power, his breath and fire and inspiration from within; not by drawing but by driving; not by shewing them what to do but by himself within them doing it. His mighty breath ran with roaring in their ears, his fire flamed in tongues upon their foreheads, and their hearts and lips were filled with himself, with the Holy Ghost. And they went forth and he went forth in them to convince the world. Hear a sample of how he convinces it. St. Peter spoke to the multitude, a crowd well representing the world, for there were men there, it is said, from every nation under heaven. At the end of his speaking 3000 souls were added to the Church. Three thousand were at one stroke convinced: here was a beginning of the world's being convinced and converted indeed. Hear too how it was done. First he told them that Jesus of Nazareth, a man marked by miracles with the stamp of God's approval, they had put to death: here then they were convinced of *their sin* because they had not believed in Christ. Then he said that this same Jesus God had raised again, that he had gone up to heaven, and that it was he who had that very day poured out the Holy Ghost: here then they were convinced of *Christ's justice,* because he had gone to the Father and could be seen no more. Lastly he bid them save themselves from that wicked generation, and they obeyed: they were then convinced that the world they had belonged to was doing the Devil's work and condemned like him; they were convinced what God's judgment on the world was, because its prince was Satan, and he was already judged.

And now, brethren, time fails me. Else I would shew you how the Holy Ghost has followed and will follow up this first beginning, convincing and converting nation after nation and age after age till the whole earth is hereafter to be covered, if only for a time, still to be covered with the knowledge of the Lord. I should shew too the manner of his convincing the world, the thousand thousand tongues he speaks by and his countless ways of working, drawing much more than I have drawn from my mysterious text, but I must forbear: yet by silence or by speech to him be glory who with the Father and the Son lives and reigns for ever and ever. Amen.

FOR MONDAY EVENING OCT. 25 1880
on Divine Providence and the Guardian Angels
THE 24TH BEING THE FEAST OF ST. RAPHAEL
(I have preached on Monday the 4th and the 11th also,
but could put down no notes)

Notes—God knows infinite things, all things, and heeds them all in particular. We cannot "do two things at once," that is cannot give our full heed and attention to two things at once. God heeds all things at once. He takes more interest in a merchant's business than the merchant, in a vessel's steering than the pilot, in a lover's sweetheart than the

[In consequence of this word *sweetheart* I was in a manner suspended and at all events was forbidden (it was some time after) to preach without having my sermon revised. However when I was going to take the next sermon I had to give after this regulation came into force to Fr. Clare for revision he poohpoohed the matter and would not look at it]

lover, in a sick man's pain than the sufferer, in our salvation than we ourselves. The hairs of our heads are numbered before him. He heeds all things and cares about all things, but not alike; he does not care for nor love nor provide for all alike, not for little things so much as great, brutes as men, the bad as the good, the reprobate who will not come to him as the elect who will. It was his law that the ox should not be muzzled that trod out the corn, but this provision was made for an example to men, not for the sake of the beast; for: Does God care for oxen? asks St. Paul; that is to say, compared with his care for men he does not care for them. Yet he does care for them and for every bird and beast and finds them their food. Not a sparrow, our Lord says, falls to the ground without your Father, that is /

without his noticing and allowing and meaning it. But we men, he added, are worth many, that is / any number of, sparrows. So then God heeds all things and cares and provides for all things but for us men he cares most and provides best.

Therefore all the things we see are made and provided for us, the sun, moon, and other heavenly bodies to light us, warm us, and be measures to us of time; coal and rockoil for artificial light and heat; animals and vegetables for our food and clothing; rain, wind, and snow again to make these bear and yield their tribute to us; water and the juices of plants for our drink; air for our breathing; stone and timber for our lodging; metals for our tools and traffic; the songs of birds, flowers and their smells and colours, fruits and their taste for our enjoyment. And so on: search the whole world and you will find it a million-million fold contrivance of providence planned for our use and patterned for our admiration.

But yet this providence is imperfect, plainly imperfect. The sun shines too long and withers the harvest, the rain is too heavy and rots it or in floods spreading washes it away; the air and water carry in their currents the poison of disease; there are poison plants, venomous snakes and scorpions; the beasts our subjects rebel, not only the bloodthirsty tiger that slaughters yearly its thousands, but even the bull will gore and the stallion bite or strike; at night the moon sometimes has no light to give, at others the clouds darken her; she measures time most strangely and gives us reckonings most difficult to make and never exact enough; the coalpits and oil-wells are full of explosions, fires, and outbreaks of sudden death, the sea of storms and wrecks, the snow has avalanches, the earth land-slips; we contend with cold, want, weakness, hunger, disease, death, and often we fight a losing battle, never a triumphant one; every-thing is full of fault, flaw, imperfection, shortcoming; as many marks as there are of God's wisdom in providing for us so many marks there may be set against them of more being needed still, of something having made of this very providence a shattered frame and a broken web.

Let us not now enquire, brethren, why this should be; we most sadly feel and know that so it is. But there is good in it; for if we were not forced from time to time to feel our need of God and our dependence on him, we should most of us cease to pray to him and to thank him. If he did everything we should treat him as though he did nothing, whereas now that he does not do all we are brought to remember how much he does and to ask for more. And God desires nothing so much as that his creatures should have recourse to him.

But there is one great means he has provided for every one of us to make up for the shortcomings of his general and common providence. This great and special providence is the giving each of us his guardian angel. *He has given,* the Scripture says, *his angels commands about thee, to keep thee in all thy ways.* And we learn from what our Lord said to his disciples that every child, that every human being, however low and of little account, is given in charge to a blessed and heavenly spirit, a guardian angel: *Beware,* said he, *of despising one of these little ones* (which means not only children but all who are in any other way little of or little account): *I tell you their angels always see the face of my Father in heaven* (Matt. 18:10.).

Consider, brethren, what a wonderful honour this is. We men are cared for by angels, fallen men by blissful spirits; we who are so full of the miseries of the flesh that we cannot bear at times to be in each other's presence are watched without ceasing by these glorious beings, and while they have us poor wretches in their sight they are at the same time gazing on the face of God. How much does God make of us when he will have his very courtiers, those who are about his throne, to look after us men, even the lowest amongst us! It may fill us with shame to be so honoured; it may also fill us with shame to think how we are watched and seen, for there is nothing we do but comes under the eye not of God only but of another witness besides, our guardian angel. He counts all our steps, he knows every hair of our heads, he is witness of all our good deeds and all our evil; he sees all and remembers all. Even our hearts he searches, for he sees them in the light of God's knowledge and God reveals to him all that can be of service to him in his charge and duty of leading the human being entrusted to him to the kingdom of heaven. But though he knows and remembers all the harm we have done he will not be our accuser; where he cannot help us he will be silent; he will speak but of our right deeds and plead in our defence all the good he has observed in us. His whole duty is to help us to be saved, to help us both in body and soul. We shall do well therefore to be ashamed of ourselves before our guardian angel, but not to have no other feelings than shame and dread towards him; for he is our good faithful and charitable friend, who never did and never could sleep one moment at his post, neglect the least thing that could be of service to us, or leave a stone unturned to help us all the days that we have been in his keeping. We should deeply trust him, we should reverence and love him, and often ask his aid.

Here, brethren, I must meet an objection which may be working on your minds. If everyone has so watchful and so strong a keeper at his side why is there such a thing as sudden death, as catching fever, as taking poison by mistake, as being shot or any way injured, even as a stumble or a fall, a scald or a sprain? What are the guardian angels doing that they let such things be?—To begin with, many mischiefs that might befall us our guardian angels do ward off from us: that is the first answer to be made. Next their power over us depends in part on the power we give them and by willingly putting ourselves into their hands, by expressly asking them to help us, we enable them to do so; for always God's special providences are for his special servants. They are not to save us from all the consequences of our own wickedness or folly or even from the wickedness and folly of other men; for we are our own masters, are free to act and then must take the consequences; moreover man is his brother's keeper and may be well or ill kept, as Abel was by wicked Cain not kept but killed. But the fullest answer is this—that in appointing us guardian angels God never meant they should make us proof against all the ills that flesh is heir to, that would have been to put us in some sort back into the state of Paradise which we have lost; but he meant them, accompanying us through this world of evil and mischance, sometimes warding off its blows and buffets, sometimes leaving them to fall, always to be leading us to a better; which better world, my brethren, when you have reached and with your own eyes opened look back on this you will see a work of wonderful wisdom in the guidance of your guardian angel. In the meantime God's providence is dark and we cannot hope to know the why and wherefore of all that is allowed to befall us.

However, my brethren, to confirm men's faith in God's providence through the guardian angels a record has been left in writing for us, the Book of Tobias. The Book of Job shews us the power of the fallen angel, of Satan, the Book of Tobias that of the holy angel St. Raphael; and both alike justify God's providence over his servants. We learn from one passage of this book what are the principal services which our guardian angels render us: *He has led me,* says young Tobias (12:3.), *both going and coming, safe; it was he that received the money from Gabelus; it was he that procured me my wife and restrained the evil spirit from its power over; he gave joy to her parents; me he delivered from being devoured by the fish, thee too he has made to see the light of heaven; and with all good we have been filled by him.* The guardian angels then (1) lead us in the way of salvation, conversing with us on the way, not that our ears hear them, but that many a good inspiration by which we are guided the right way or kept from the wrong comes from them. (2) They help us in our worldly business, even in money matters. (3) They bring about happy marriages. (4) They control the power of the Devil over us.

(5) They give spiritual joy. (6) They save us from death and heal us in disease. And (7) we learn from the words of St. Raphael himself (ibid. 12.) that they offer our prayers to God.

Some words on devotion to our guardian angels.

L.D.S.[23]

---

[23]*Laus Deo semper* ("Praise to God always"), a phrase often found at the end of Jesuit or Jesuit schoolboy documents.

Commentary on the *Spiritual Exercises* of St. Ignatius and Other Spiritual Writings

FIRST PRINCIPLE AND FOUNDATION

Man was created to praise, reverence and serve God Our Lord, and by so doing to save his soul. And the other things on the face of the earth were created for man's sake and to help him in the carrying out of the end for which he was created. Hence it follows that man should make use of creatures so far as they help him to attain his end and withdraw from them so far as they hinder him from so doing. For that, it is necessary to make ourselves indifferent in regard to all created things in so far as it is left to the choice of our free will and there is no prohibition; in such sort that we do not on our part seek for health rather than sickness, for riches rather than poverty, for honour rather than dishonour, for a long life rather than a short one; and so in all other things, desiring and choosing only those which may better lead us to the end for which we were created.

On *Principium sive Fundamentum*
[On Creation]

"Homo creatus est"—Aug. 20, 1880: during this retreat, which I am making at Liverpool, I have been thinking about creation and this thought has led the way naturally through the exercises hitherto. I put down some thoughts.—We may learn that all things are created by consideration of the world without or of ourselves the world within. The former is the consideration commonly dwelt on, but the latter takes on the mind more hold. I find myself both as man and as myself something most determined and distinctive, at pitch, more distinctive and higher pitched than anything else I see; I find myself with my pleasures and pains, my powers and my experiences, my deserts and guilt, my shame and sense of beauty, my dangers, hopes, fears, and all my fate, more important to myself than anything I see. And when I ask where does all this throng and stack of being, so rich, so distinctive, so important, come from / nothing I see can answer me. And this whether I speak of human nature or of my individuality, my selfbeing. For human nature, being more highly pitched, selved, and distinctive than anything in the world, can have been developed, evolved, condensed, from the vastness of the world not anyhow or by the working of common powers but only by one of finer or higher pitch and determination than itself and certainly than any that elsewhere we see, for this power had to force forward the starting or stubborn elements to the one pitch required. And this is much more true when we consider the mind; when I consider my selfbeing, my consciousness and feeling of myself, that taste of myself, of *I* and *me* above and in all things, which is more distinctive than the taste of ale or alum, more distinctive than the smell of wal-nutleaf or camphor, and is incommunicable by any means to another man (as when I was a child I used to ask myself: What must it be to be someone else?). Nothing else in nature comes near this unspeak-able stress of pitch, distinctiveness, and selving, this selfbeing of my own. Nothing explains it or resembles it, except so far as this, that other men to themselves have the same feeling. But this only multi-plies the phenomena to be explained so far as the cases are like and do resemble. But to me there is no resemblance: searching nature I taste *self* but at one tankard, that of my own being. The develop-ment, refinement, condensation of nothing shews any sign of being able to match this to me or give me another taste of it, a taste even resembling it.

[On Grace and Free Will]

This matter is profound; but so far as I see this is the truth. First, though self, as personality, is prior to nature it is not prior to pitch. If there were something prior even to pitch, of which that pitch would be itself the pitch, then we could suppose that that, like everything else, was subject to God's will and could be pitched, could be determined, this way or that. But this is really saying that a thing is and is not itself, is and is not A, is and is not. For self before nature is no thing as yet but only possible; with the accession of a nature it becomes properly a self, for instance a person: only so far as it is prior to nature, that is to say / so far as it is a definite self, the possibility of a definite self (and not merely the possibility of a number or fetch of nature) it is identified with pitch, moral pitch, determination of right and wrong. And so far, it has its possibility, as it will have its existence, from God, but not so that God makes pitch no pitch, determination no determination, and difference indifference. The indifference, the absence of pitch, is in the nature to be superadded. And when nature is superadded, then it cannot be believed, as the Thomists think, that in every circumstance of free choice the person is of himself indifferent towards the alternatives and that God determines which he shall, though freely, choose. The difficulty does not lie so much in his being determined by God and yet choosing freely, for on one side that may and must happen, but in his being supposed equally disposed or pitched towards both at once. This is impossible and destroys the notion of freedom and of pitch.

Nevertheless in every circumstance it is within God's power to determine the creature to choose, and freely choose, according to his will; but not without a change or access of circumstance, over and above the bare act of determination on his part. This access is either of grace, which is "supernature," to nature or of more grace to grace already given, and it takes the form of instressing the affective will, of affecting the will towards the good which he proposes. So far this is a necessary and constrained affection on the creature's part, to which the *arbitrium* of the creature may give its avowal and consent. Ordinarily when grace is given we feel first the necessary or constrained act and after that the free act on our own part, of consent or refusal as the case may be. This consent or refusal is given to an act either hereafter or now to be done, but in the nature of things such an act must always be future, even if immediately future or of those futures which arise in acts and phrases like "I must ask you" to do so-and-so, "I wish to apologise," "I beg to say," and so on. And ordinarily the motives for refusal are still present though the motive for consent has been strengthened by the motion, just over or even in some way still working, of grace. And therefore in ordinary cases refusal is possible not only physically but also morally and often takes place. But refusal remaining physically possible becomes morally (and strictly) impossible in the following way.

Besides the above stated distinction of freedom of pitch and freedom of play there is a third kind of freedom still to be considered, *freedom of field*. (This is the natural order of the three: freedom of pitch, that is / self determination, is in the chooser himself and his choosing faculty; freedom of play is in the execution; freedom of field is in the object, the field of choice.) Thus it is freedom of play to be free of some benevolent man's purse, to have access to it at your will; it is freedom of pitch to be allowed to take from it what you want, not to be limited by conditions of his imposing; it is freedom of field to find there *more than one coin to choose from*. Or it is freedom of pitch to be able to choose for yourself which of several doors you will go in by; it is freedom of play to go unhindered to it and through the one you choose; but suppose all were false doors or locked but the very one you happened to choose and you do not know it, there is here wanting freedom of field.

It has been shewn . . . how God can always command if he chooses the free consent of the elective will, at least, if by no other way, by shutting out all freedom of field (which no doubt does sometimes take place, as in disposing the hearts of princes; but whether in matters concerning the subject's own salvation we do not know: very possibly it does in answer to the subject's own or some other's prayer in his behalf). Therefore in that "cleave" of being which each of his creatures shews to God's eyes alone (or in its "burl" of being / uncloven) God can choose countless points in the strain (or countless cleaves of the "burl") where the creature has consented, does consent, to God's will in the way above shewn. But these may be away, may be very far away, from the actual pitch at any given moment existing. It is into that possible world that God for the moment moves his creature out of this one or it is from that possible world that he brings his creature into this, shewing it to itself gracious and consenting; nay more, clothing its old self for the moment with a gracious and consenting self. This shift is grace. For grace is any action, activity, on God's part by which, in creating or after creating, he carries the creature to or towards the end of its being, which is its selfsacrifice to God and its salvation. It is, I say, any such activity on God's part; so that so far as this action or activity is God's it is divine stress, holy spirit, and, as all is done through Christ, Christ's spirit; so far as it is action, correspondence, on the creature's it is *actio salutaris;* so far as it is looked at *in esse quieto* it is Christ in his member on the one side, his member in Christ on the other. It is as if a man said: That is Christ playing at me and me playing at Christ, only that it is no play but truth; That is Christ *being me* and me being Christ.

[Christ's Grace]

God's forestalling of man's action by prevenient grace, which carries with it a consenting of man's will, seems to stand to the action of free choice which follows and to which, by its continued strain and breathing on and man's responding aspiration or drawing in of breath, it leads / as the creation of man and angels in sanctifying grace stands to the act by which they entered with God into the covenant and commonwealth of original justice; further / as the infused

virtues of baptism stand to the acts of faith etc which long after fol-
low. This agrees well with the light I once had upon the nature of
faith, that it is God / in man / knowing his own truth. It is like the
child of a great nobleman taught by its father and mother a compli-
ment of welcome to pay to the nobleman's father on his visit to them:
the child does not understand the words it says by rote, does not
know their meaning, yet what they mean it means. The parents
understand what they do not say, the child says what it does not
understand, but both child and parents mean the welcome.

The will is surrounded by the objects of desire as the needle by the
points of the compass. It has play then in two dimensions. This is to
say / it is drawn by affection towards any one, A, and this freely, and
it can change its direction towards any other, as free, B, which
implies the moving through an arc. It has in fact, more or less, in its
affections a tendency of magnetism towards every object and the
arbitrium, the elective will, decides which: this is the needle proper.
But in fallen man all this motion, both these dimensions, κεῖται ἐν
τῷ πονηρῷ; so that the uplifting action of supernatural grace takes
place as if in a third dimension, motion, in which man is totally inca-
pable. And here remark what now clearly appears, that the action of
such assisting grace is twofold, to help man determine the will
towards the right object in one field and at the same time from that
field or plane to lift it to a parallel and higher one; besides all the
while stimulating its action, in the right plane and in the right direc-
tion, towards the right object; so that in fact it is threefold, not
twofold—(1) quickening, stimulating, towards the object, towards
good: this is especially in the affective will, might be a natural grace,
and in a high degree seems to be the grace of novices; (2) corrective,
turning the will from one direction or pitting into another, like the
needle through an arc, determining its choice (I mean / stimulating
that determination, which it still leaves free): this touches the elective
will or the power of election and is especially the grace of the mature

mind; (3) elevating, which lifts the receiver from one cleave of being to another and to a vital act in Christ: this is truly God's finger touching the very vein of personality, which nothing else can reach and man can respond to by no play whatever, by bare acknowledgment only, the counter stress which God alone can feel ("subito probas eum"), the aspiration in answer to his inspiration. Of this I have written above and somewhere else long ago.

When man was created in grace, that is / in the elevated, the supernatural / state, and his will addressed towards God, the work of actual grace was all of the first sort. This may be called creative grace, the grace which destined the victim for the sacrifice, and which belongs to God the Father. After the Fall there came too "medicinal," corrective, redeeming / grace, by the restrictions of the Law, by the exhortations of the Prophets, and by Christ himself. And all Christ's words, it seems to me, are either words of cure, as "Veniam et curabo eum," "Volo, mundare," or corrections of some error or fault; their function is always *ramener à la route*. This then is especially Christ's grace, it is a purifying and a mortifying grace, bringing the victim to the altar and sacrificing it. And as creative grace became insufficient by the Fall: so this grace of Christ's did not avail when he was no longer present to keep bestowing it or when its first force was spent. At Pentecost the elevating grace was given which fastened men in good. This is especially the grace of the Holy Ghost and is the acceptance and assumption of the victim of the sacrifice.

[Contemplation on Love]

The last mystery meditated on in the Spiritual Exercises is our Lord's Ascension. This contemplation is that which comes next in order, namely the sending of the Holy Ghost; it is the contemplation of the Holy Ghost sent to us through creatures. Observe then it is on love and the Holy Ghost is called Love ("Fons vivus, ignis, *caritas*");

shewn "in operibus," the works of God's finger ("Digitus paternae dexterae"); consisting "in communicatione" etc, and the Holy Ghost as he is the bond and mutual love of Father and Son, so of God and man; that the Holy Ghost is uncreated grace and the sharing by man of the divine nature and the bestowal of himself by God on man ("Altissimi donum Dei"): hence we are to consider "quantum . . . Dominus desideret dare seipsum mihi in quantum potest"; hence also the repetition in pt. 2 of "dans." Remark also how after the benefits of creation and Redemption he does not add, he means *us* to add, that of sanctification. Again in Pt. 2 "templum," in 3. "operatur" as above, in 4. "a sole . . . radii, a fonte aquae" ("*Fons* vivus, *ignis*") (Dec. 8 1881). All things therefore are charged with love, are charged with God and if we know how to touch them give off sparks and take fire, yield drops and flow, ring and tell of him.

CREATION AND REDEMPTION
THE GREAT SACRIFICE

Nov. 8 1881 (*Long Retreat*)

Time has 3 dimensions and one positive pitch or direction. It is therefore not so much like any river or any sea as like the Sea of Galilee, which has the Jordan running through it and giving a current to the whole.

Though this one direction of time if prolonged for ever might be considered to be parallel to or included in the duration of God, the same might be said of any other direction in time artificially taken. But it is truer to say that there is no relation between any duration of time and the duration of God. And in no case is it to be supposed that God creates time and the things of time, that is to say / this world, in that duration of himself which is parallel with the duration of time and was before time. But rather as the light falls from heaven upon the Sea of Galilee not only from the north, from which quarter the Jordan comes, but from everywhere / so God from every point, so to say, of his being creates all things. But in so far as the creation of one thing depends on that of another, as suppose trees were created *for* man and *before* man, so far does God create in time or in the direction or duration of time.

There is therefore in the works of creation an order of time, as the order of the Six Days, and another order, the order of intention, and that not only intention in understanding and intention in will but also intention or forepitch of execution, of power or activity. In the order of intention "other things on the face of the earth" are created after man; the more perfect first, the less after. From this it follows that the more perfect is created in its perfection, that is to say / if perfectible and capable of greater and less perfection, it is created at its greatest. And thus it is said "Ipsius enim sumus factura, *creati in Christo Jesu* in operibus bonis, quae praeparavit Deus ut in illis ambulemus" (Eph. 2:10., and he had already dwelt on these Gentiles and on himself too as having been children of wrath, dead in sins, and so on). And further it follows that man himself was created for Christ as Christ's created nature for God (cf. "omnia enim vestra sunt, vos autem Christi, Christus autem Dei" I Cor. 3:22, 23.). And in this way Christ is the firstborn among creatures. The elect then were created in Christ some before his birth, as Abraham, some before their own, as St. Ignatius; that so their correspondence with grace and seconding of God's designs is like a taking part in their own creation, the creation of their best selves. And again the wicked and the lost are like halfcreations and have but a halfbeing.

The first intention then of God outside himself or, as they say, *ad extra,* outwards, the first outstress of God's power, was Christ; and we must believe that the next was the Blessed Virgin. Why did the

Son of God go thus forth from the Father not only in the eternal and intrinsic procession of the Trinity but also by an extrinsic and less than eternal, let us say aeonian one?—To give God glory and that by sacrifice, sacrifice offered in the barren wilderness outside of God, as the children of Israel were led into the wilderness to offer sacrifice. This sacrifice and this outward procession is a consequence and shadow of the procession of the Trinity, from which mystery sacrifice takes its rise; but of this I do not mean to write here. It is as if the blissful agony or stress of selving in God had forced out drops of sweat or blood, which drops were the world, or as if the lights lit at the festival of the "peaceful Trinity" through some little cranny striking out lit up into being one "cleave"out of the world of possible creatures. The sacrifice would be the Eucharist, and that the victim might be truly victim like, like motionless, helpless, or lifeless, it must be in matter. Then the Blessed Virgin was intended or predestined to minister that matter. And here then was that mystery of the woman clothed with the sun which appeared in heaven. She followed Christ the nearest, following the sacrificial lamb "whithersoever he went."

In going forth to do sacrifice Christ went not alone but created angels to be his company, lambs to follow him the Lamb, the flower of the flock, "whithersoever he went," that is to say, first to the hill of sacrifice, then after that back to God, to beatitude. They were to take part in the sacrifice and he was to redeem them all, that is to say / for the sake of the Lamb of God who was God himself God would accept the whole flock and for the sake of one ear or grape the whole sheaf or cluster; for redeem may be said not only of the recovering from sin to grace or perdition to salvation but also of the raising from worthlessness before God (and all creation is unworthy of God) to worthiness of him, the meriting of God himself, or, so to say, godworthiness. In this sense the Blessed Virgin was beyond all others redeemed, because it was her more than all other creatures that Christ meant to win from nothingness and it was her that he meant to raise the highest.

Christ then like a good shepherd led the way; but when Satan saw the mystery and the humiliation proposed he turned back and rebelled or, as that Welsh text says, flung himself direct on beatitude, to seize it of his own right and merit and by his own strength, and so he fell, with his following.

Here I have thought of a parable of a marriage cavalcade, in which some as soon as they see the bride's lowly dwelling refuse to go further, are themselves disowned by the bridegroom and driven off, but keep attacking the procession on its road.

The mystery remained in some sort a mystery. When Satan saw Mary and Christ in the flesh he did not recognize them. This may be the meaning of the woman's hiding in the wilderness, that is / the material world. The river that the dragon vomited to sweep the woman away perhaps means that Satan, who is the κοσμοκράτωρ, the worldwielder, gave nature all an impulse of motion which should destroy human life, and the earth's helping the woman and swallowing the river that nature absorbed this motion and was overruled to digest and distribute it throughout, making it still habitable by man. I understand the sun, moon, and stars to mean two things—first to compare the woman to the earth, this planet, which is clothed in sunlight, ministered to more humbly by its satellite, and graced by the beauty of the zodiac and other signs of the firmament, and then to her being adorned with God's grace, the service of material nature below, and the service of angels above. By the "other sign that appeared in heaven," of the red or fiery dragon I understand the counterpageant or counterstandard set up by Lucifer which reduced a third of the angels and he is said with his tail to have swept the third part of the stars down to the earth because he drew them in his train and they were involved in his fall, not that he cast them down before himself. As the woman is compared to the earth in the solar system so the dragon is to the constellation Draco, the tail of which sweeps through 120° or a third of the sphere and which winds round the pole (the polestar was once in the head of Draco, I mean a star in the head of Draco was then the polestar), this world's seeming axis and the earth's real one, so as to symbolise how Satan tried to possess himself of the sovereignty of things, taking "The mountain of the North," that is to say / the culmination of the firmament towards the pole, as a throne and post of vantage and so wreathing nature and as it were constricting it to his purposes (as also he wreathed himself in the Garden round the Tree of Knowledge); though he was foiled, cast from heaven, and left master only of the material world, by a figure the earth.

A coil or spiral is then a type of the Devil, who is called the old (or original) serpent, and this I suppose because of its "swale" or subtle and imperceptible drawing in towards its head or centre, and it is a type of death, of motion lessening and at last ceasing. *Invidia autem diaboli mors intravit in mumdum:* God gave things a forward and perpetual motion; the Devil, that is / thrower of things off the track, upsetter, mischiefmaker, clashing one with another brought in the law of decay and consumption in inanimate nature, death in the vegetable and animal world, moral death and original sin in the world of man. This seems to expand the meaning of that river explained on last leaf and also of the river running through the lake spoken of. . . .

The snake or serpent a symbol of the Devil. So also the Dragon. A dragon is or is taken to be a reptile. And first a dragon is a serpent with any addition you make, as of feet or of wings or something less. I found some Greek proverb "The serpent till he has devoured a serpent does not become a dragon" and the snakes found in China and preserved in temples for adoration are called dragons in virtue of some supposed incarnation which has taken place in them, but they are and look ordinary snakes. So that if the Devil is symbolized as a snake he must be an archsnake and a dragon. Mostly dragons are represented as much more than serpents, but always as in some way reptiles. Now among the vertebrates the reptiles go near to combine the qualities of the other classes in themselves and are, I think, taken by the Evolutionists as nearest the original vertebrate stem and as the point of departure for the rest. In this way clearly dragons are represented as gathering up the attributes of many creatures: they are reptiles always, but besides sometimes have bat's wings; four legs, sometimes those of the mammal quadrupeds, sometimes birds' feet and talons; jaws sometimes of crocodiles, but sometimes of eagles; armouring like crocodiles again, but also sturgeons and other fish, or lobsters and other crustacea; or like insects; colours like the dragonfly and other insects; sometimes horns; and so on. And therefore I suppose the dragon as a type of the Devil to express the universality of his powers, both the gifts he has by nature and the attributes and sway he grasps, and the horror which the whole inspires. We must of course remember how the Cherubim are in Scripture represented as composite beings, combinations of eagles, lions, oxen, and men, and that the religions of heathendom have sphinxes, fauns and satyrs, "eyas-gods," "the dog-Anubis," and so on. The dragon then symbolizes one who aiming at every perfection ends by being a monster, a "fright."

The word Throne, one of the nine choirs, suggests that the rebel angels might claim that the sacrifice should be offered in them as living altars, not on earth or in anything earthly. Satan sets up a rival altar and sacrifice, which did not please, any more than those of Cain or of Core, and fire, as with Core, broke out from below. Whereas the manchild to whom the woman gives birth is, like a pleasing sacrifice, caught up to God's throne.

INSTRUCTIONS

The principle or foundation

Homo creatus est—CREATION THE MAKING OUT OF NOTHING, bringing from nothing into being: once there was nothing, then lo, this huge world was there. How great a work of power!

The loaf is made with flour; the house with bricks; the plough, the cannon, the locomotive, the warship / of iron—all of things that were before, of matter; but the world, with the flour, the grain, the wheatear, the seed, the ground, the sun, the rain; with the bricks, the clay, the earth; with the iron and the mine, the fuel and the furnace, was made from nothing. And they are MADE IN TIME AND WITH LABOUR, the world in no time with a word. MAN CANNOT CREATE a single speck, God creates all that is besides himself.

But MEN OF GENIUS ARE SAID TO CREATE, a painting, a poem, a tale, a tune, a policy; not indeed the colours and the canvas, not the words or notes, but the design, the character, the air, the plan. How then?—from themselves, from their own minds. And they themselves, their minds and all, are creatures of God: if the tree created much more the flower and the fruit.

To know what creation is LOOK AT THE SIZE OF THE WORLD. Speed of light: it would fly six or seven times round the earth while the clock ticks once. Yet it takes *thousands of years* to reach us from the Milky Way, which is made up of stars swarming together (though as far from one another as we are from some of them), running into one, and looking like a soft mist, and each of them a million times as big as the earth perhaps (the sun is about that). And there is not the least reason to think that is anything like the size of the whole world. And all arose at a word! So that the greatest of all works in the world, nay the world itself, was easier made than the least little thing that man or any other creature makes in the world.

WHY DID GOD CREATE?—Not for sport, not for nothing. Every sensible man has a purpose in all he does, every workman has a use for every object he makes. Much more has God a purpose, an end, a meaning in his work. He meant the world to give him praise, reverence, and service; *to give him glory.* It is like a garden, a field he sows: what should it bear him? praise, reverence, and service; it should yield him glory. It is an estate he farms: what should it bring him in? Praise, reverence, and service; it should repay him glory. It is a leasehold he lets out: what should its rent be? Praise, reverence, and service; its rent is his glory. It is a bird he teaches to sing, a pipe, a harp he plays on: what should it sing to him? etc. It is a glass he looks in: what should it shew him? With praise, reverence, and service it should shew him his own glory. It is a book he has written, of the riches of his knowledge, teaching endless truths, full lessons of wisdom, a poem of beauty: what is it about? His praise, the reverence due to him, the way to serve him; it tells him of his glory. It is a censer fuming: what is the sweet incense? His praise, his reverence, his service; it rises to his glory. It is an altar and a victim on it lying in his sight: why is it offered? To his praise, honour, and service: it is a sacrifice to his glory.

The creation does praise God, does reflect honour on him, is of service to him, and yet the praises fall short; the honour is like none, less than a buttercup to a king; the service is of no service to him. In other words *he does not need it.* He has infinite glory without it and what is infinite can be made no bigger. Nevertheless he takes it: he wishes it, asks it, he commands it, he enforces it, he gets it.

The sun and the stars shining glorify God. They stand where he placed them, they move where he bid them. "The heavens declare the glory of God." They glorify God, *but they do not know it.* The birds sing to him, the thunder speaks of his terror, the lion is like his strength, the sea is like his greatness, the honey like his sweetness; they are something like him, they make him known, they tell of him, they give him glory, but they do not know they do, they do not know him, they never can, they are brute things that only think of food or think of nothing. This then is poor praise, faint reverence, slight service, dull glory. Nevertheless what they can *they always do.*

But AMIDST THEM ALL IS MAN, man and the angels: we will speak of man. Man was created. Like the rest then to praise, reverence, and serve God; to give him glory. He does so, even by his being, beyond all visible creatures: "What a piece of work is man!" (Expand by "Domine, Dominus, quam admirabile etc . . . Quid est homo . . . Minuisti eum paulo minus ab angelis.") But man can know God, *can mean to give him glory.* This then was why he was made, to give God glory and to mean to give it; to praise God fréely, wíllingly to reverence him, gládly to serve him. Man was made to give, and mean to give, God glory.

I WAS MADE FOR THIS, each one of us was made for this.

Does man then do it? Never mind others now nor the race of man: DO I DO IT?—If I sin I do not: how can I dishonour God and honour him? willfully dishonour him and yet be meaning to honour him? choose to disobey him and mean to serve him? No, we have not answered God's purposes, we have not reached the end of our being. Are we God's orchard or God's vineyard? we have yielded rotten fruit, sour grapes, or none. Are we his cornfield sown? we have not come to ear or are mildewed in the ear. Are we his farm? it is a losing one to him. Are we his tenants? we have refused him rent. Are we his singing bird? we will not learn to sing. Are we his pipe or harp? we are out of tune, we grate upon his ear. Are we his glass to look in? we are deep in dust or our silver gone or we are broken or, worst of all, we misshape his face and make God's image hideous. Are we his book? we are blotted, we are scribbled over with foulness and blasphemy. Are we his censer? we breathe stench and not sweetness. Are we his sacrifice? we are like the sacrifice of Balac, of Core, and of Cain. If we have sinned we are all this.

But what we have not done yet we can do now, what we have done badly hitherto we can do well henceforward, we can repent our sins and BEGIN TO GIVE GOD GLORY. The moment we do this we reach the end of our being, we do and are what we were made for, we make it worth God's while to have created us. This is a comforting thought: we need not wait in fear till death; any day, any minute we bless God for our being or for anything, for food, for sunlight, we do and are what we were meant for, made for—things that give and mean to give God glory. This is a thing to live for. Then make haste so to live.

For IF YOU ARE IN SIN YOU ARE GOD'S ENEMY, you cannot love or praise him. You may say you are far from hating God; but if you live in sin you are among God's enemies, you are under Satan's standard and enlisted there; you may not like it, no wonder; you may wish to be elsewhere; but there you are, an enemy to God. It is indeed better to praise him than blaspheme, but the praise is not a hearty praise; it cannot be. You cannot mean your praise if while praise is on the lips there is no reverence in the mind; there can be no reverence in the mind if there is no obedience, no submission, no service. And there can be no obeying God while you disobey him, no service while you sin. Turn then, brethren, now and give God glory. You do say grace at meals and thank and praise God for your daily bread, so far so good, but thank and praise him now for everything. When a man is in God's grace and free from mortal sin, then everything that he does, so long as there is no sin in it, gives God glory and what does not give him glory has some, however little, sin in it. It is not only prayer that gives God glory but work. Smiting on an anvil, sawing a beam, whitewashing a wall, driving horses, sweeping, scouring, everything gives God some glory if being in his grace you do it as your duty. To go to communion worthily gives God great glory, but to take food in thankfulness and temperance gives him glory too. To lift up the hands in prayer gives God glory, but a man with a dungfork in his hand, a woman with a sloppail, give him glory too. He is so great that all things give him glory if you mean they should. So then, my brethren, live.

SUGGESTIONS
FOR FURTHER READING

BERGONZI, BERNARD. *Gerard Manley Hopkins.* New York: Macmillan, 1977.

BUMP, JEROME. *Gerard Manley Hopkins.* Boston: Twayne Publishers, 1982.

COTTER, JAMES FINN. *Inscape: The Christology and Poetry of Gerard Manley Hopkins.* Pittsburgh, Pa.: University of Pittsburgh Press, 1972.

DOWNES, DAVID ANTHONY. *The Ignatian Personality of Gerard Manley Hopkins.* Lanham, Md.: University Press of America, 1990.

DUNS SCOTUS, JOHN. *Philosophical Writings: A Selection.* Trans., with intro. and notes by Allan Wolter. 2d ed. Indianapolis: Hackett, 1987.

ELLIS, VIRGINIA RIDLEY. *Gerard Manley Hopkins and the Language of Mystery.* Columbia: University of Missouri Press, 1991.

ELLSBERG, MARGARET R. *Created to Praise: The Language of Gerard Manley Hopkins.* Oxford: Oxford University Press, 1987.

GARDNER, W. H. *Gerard Manley Hopkins, 1884–1889: A Study of Poetic Idiosyncrasy in Relation to Poetic Tradition.* 2 vols. London: Secker and Warburg, 1949.

HARRIS, DANIEL. *Inspirations Unbidden: The "Terrible" Sonnets of Gerard Manley Hopkins.* Berkeley: University of California Press, 1982.

HARTMANN, GEOFFREY H. *The Unmediated Vision: An Interpretation of Wordsworth, Hopkins, Rilke and Valéry.* New York: Harcourt Brace & World, 1966.

HAUSER, ALAN. *The Shaping Vision of Gerard Manley Hopkins.* London: Oxford University Press, 1958.

HOPKINS, GERARD MANLEY. *The Correspondence of Gerard Manley Hopkins and Richard Watson Dixon.* Ed. C. C. Abbott, 1935. Rev. ed. London: Oxford University Press, 1955.

———. *The Early Poetic Manuscripts and Note-Books of Gerard Manley Hopkins in Facsimile.* Ed. Norman H. McKenzie. New York: Garland, 1989.

———. *Further Letters of Gerard Manley Hopkins Including His Correspondence with Coventry Patmore.* Ed. C. C. Abbott, 1938. Rev. ed. London: Oxford University Press, 1956.

———. *The Journals and Papers of Gerard Manley Hopkins.* Ed. Humphrey House; completed by Graham Storey. London: Oxford University Press, 1959.

———. *The Later Poetic Manuscripts of Gerard Manley Hopkins in Facsimile.* Ed. Norman H. MacKenzie. New York: Garland, 1991.

———. *The Letters of Gerard Manley Hopkins to Robert Bridges.* Ed. C. C. Abbott, 1935. Rev. ed. London: Oxford University Press, 1955.

———. *The Oxford Authors: Gerard Manley Hopkins.* Ed. Catherine Phillips. London: Oxford University Press, 1986.

———. *Poems of Gerard Manley Hopkins.* Ed. Robert Bridges. London: Humphrey Milford, 1918.

———. *The Poetical Works of Gerard Manley Hopkins.* Ed. Norman MacKenzie. Oxford: Clarendon, 1990.

———. *The Sermons and Devotional Writings of Gerard Manley Hopkins.* Ed. Christopher Devlin, 1959. London: Oxford University Press, 1967.

JOHNSON, WENDELL STACY. *Gerard Manley Hopkins: The Poet as Victorian.* Ithaca, N.Y.: Cornell University Press, 1968.

THE KENYON CRITICS (Austin Warren, Marshall McLuhan, et al). *Gerard Manley Hopkins.* New York: New Directions, 1945.

KUHN, JOAQUIN, AND JOSEPH J. FEENEY, S.J., eds. *Hopkins Variations: Standing Round a Waterfall*. Philadelphia: Saint Joseph's University Press; and New York: Fordham University Press, 2002.

MCKENZIE, NORMAN. *A Reader's Guide to Gerard Manley Hopkins*. Ithaca, N.Y.: Cornell University Press, 1981.

MARIANI, PAUL. *A Commentary on the Complete Poems of Gerard Manley Hopkins*. Ithaca, N.Y.: Cornell University Press, 1970.

MARTIN, ROBERT BERNARD. *Gerard Manley Hopkins: A Very Private Life*. New York: Putnam, 1991.

MILLER, J. HILLIS. "Gerard Manley Hopkins." In *The Disappearance of God: Five Nineteenth-Century Writers*. New York: Schocken, 1965, 270–359.

MILROY, JAMES. *The Language of Gerard Manley Hopkins*. London: André Deutsch, 1977.

MILWARD, PETER, AND RAYMOND V. SCHODER. *Landscape and Inscape: Vision and Inspiration in Hopkins's Poetry*. Grand Rapids, Mich.: Eerdmans, 1975.

NIXON, JUDE. *Gerard Manley Hopkins and His Contemporaries: Liddon, Newman, Darwin, and Pater*. New York: Garland, 1994.

PHILLIPS, CATHERINE. *Robert Bridges: A Biography*. Oxford: Oxford University Press, 1992.

RITZ, JEAN-GEORGE. *Robert Bridges and Gerard Hopkins, 1863–1889: A Literary Friendship*. London: Oxford University Press, 1960.

ROBINSON, JOHN. *In Extremity: A Study of Gerard Manley Hopkins*. Cambridge: Cambridge University Press, 1978.

SAVILLE, JULIA F. *A Queer Chivalry: The Homoerotic Asceticism of Gerard Manley Hopkins*. Charlottesville: University Press of Virginia, 2000.

SCHNEIDER, ELIZABETH. *The Dragon in the Gate: Studies in the Poetry of Gerard Manley Hopkins*. Berkeley and Los Angeles: University of California Press, 1968.

SPRINKER, MICHAEL. *"A Counterpoint of Dissonance": The Aesthetics and Poetry of Gerard Manley Hopkins.* Baltimore, Md.: Johns Hopkins University Press, 1980.

SULLOWAY, ALISON. *Gerard Manley Hopkins and the Victorian Temper.* New York: Columbia University Press, 1972.

THORNTON, R. K. R., ed. *All My Eyes See: The Visual World of Gerard Manley Hopkins.* Sunderland: Coelfrith Press, 1975.

———. *Gerard Manley Hopkins: The Poems.* London: Edward Arnold, 1973.

WALHOUT, DONALD. *Send My Roots Rain: A Study of Religious Experience in the Poetry of Gerard Manley Hopkins.* Athens: Ohio University Press, 1981.

WHITE, NORMAN. *Hopkins: A Literary Biography.* Oxford: Clarendon, 1992.

Across my foundering deck shone
A beacon, an eternal beam. | Flesh fade, and mortal trash
Fall to the residuary worm; | world's wildfire, leave but ash:
In a flash, at a trumpet crash,
I am all at once what Christ is, | since he was what I am, and
This Jack, joke, poor potsherd, | patch, matchwood immortal
diamond,
Is immortal diamond.

—*concluding lines from* "That Nature is a Heraclitean Fire
and of the comfort of the Resurrection"

ACKNOWLEDGMENTS

The editors of this book wish gratefully to acknowledge the reprinting of the following, by permission of Oxford University Press:

1. *From* Gerard Manley Hopkins, *Gerard Manley Hopkins: The Major Works,* edited and with an introduction and notes by Catherine Phillips. New York: Oxford, Oxford World's Classics edn., 1986, 2002; Poems © the Society of Jesus 1986, 2002, *the following:*

Poetry

"Heaven-Haven (a nun takes the veil)," "The Habit of Perfection," *"Nondum," "Oratio Patris Condren: O Jesu vivens in Maria," "S. Thomae Aquinatis: Rhythmus ad SS. Sacramentum,"* "The Wreck of the Deutschland," "God's Grandeur," "The Starlight Night," "The Sea and the Skylark," "As kingfishers catch fire," "Spring," "The Windhover: to Christ our Lord," "Pied Beauty," "The Caged Skylark," "Hurrahing in Harvest," "The Lantern out of Doors," "The Loss of the Eurydice," "Duns Scotus's Oxford," "Henry Purcell," "The Bugler's First Communion," "Binsey Poplars," "Felix Randal," "Spring and Fall: to a Young Child," "The Leaden Echo and the Golden Echo (Maidens' song from *St. Winefred's Well*)," "Ribblesdale," "The Blessed Virgin compared to the Air we Breathe," "I wake and feel," "No worst," "To what serves Mortal Beauty?," "(Carrion Comfort)," "(The Soldier)," "Thee, God, I come from," "My own heart," "Spelt from Sibyl's Leaves," "Harry Ploughman," "That

Nature is a Heraclitean Fire and of the comfort of the Resurrection," "In honour of St. Alphonsus Rodriguez," *"Justus quidem tu es, Domine"*

Prose

P. 185, [Oxford, 1863]: "Flick, fillip, flip, fleck, flake."; *p. 189,* January 23, 1866: "For Lent. No pudding on Sundays"; *pp. 191–2,* "[1866] July 17. Dull . . . cog their woody twigs"; *pp. 193–97,* "[Holiday in Switzerland] . . . valley red in the sunset"; *pp. 203–9,* "[1871] The spring weather began . . . was carried out"; *pp. 215–17,* "[1873] Feb. 24, 1873—In the snow . . . it were left in them"; *pp. 162–63,* Oct. 15, 1866: To the Rev. Dr. John H. Newman; *pp. 223–26,* Oct. 16, 1866: To his father; *pp. 227–29,* Aug. 21, 1877: To Robert Bridges; *pp. 232–34,* May 30, 1878: To Robert Bridges; *pp. 240–41,* Oct. 25, 1879: To Robert Bridges; *pp. 249,* Oct. 29, 1881: To R.W. Dixon; *pp. 250–54,* Dec. 1, 1881: To R.W. Dixon; *pp. 259–60,* March 7, 1884: To Robert Bridges; *p. 343,* May 8, 1889: To his mother

2. *From* Gerard Manley Hopkins, *The Sermons and Devotional Writings of Gerard Manley Hopkins,* edited by Christopher Devlin, S.J. London: Oxford University Press, 1959, *the following:*

Pp. 17–18, Sunday, August 17, 1879: Cure of the Deaf and Dumb Man (Mark 7:31–37); *pp. 30–32,* Sunday, Nov. 9, 1879: On the Healing of Jairus' Daughter and the Woman with the Issue of Blood (Matt. 9:18–26; Mark 5:22; Luke 8:41); *pp. 34–38,* Sunday, Nov. 23, 1879: On Jesus Christ as Our Hero (Luke 2:33); *pp. 46–49,* Sunday, Dec. 14, 1879: "Rejoice in the Lord always" (Phil. 4:4, 5); *pp. 68–75,* Sunday, April 25, 1880: The Paraclete (John 16:5–14); *pp. 89–93,* Sunday, Oct. 25, 1880: On Divine Providence and the Guardian Angels; *pp. 122–23,* "First Principle and Foundation . . . a taste even resembling it"; *pp. 148–49,* "This matter is profound . . . freedom of field"; "It has been shewn . . . and me being Christ"; *pp. 157–58,*

"God's forestalling of man's action . . . victim of the sacrifice"; *p. 195,* "The last mystery . . . ring and tell of him"; *pp. 196–99,* "Creation and Redemption . . . up to God's throne"; *pp. 238–41* "Instructions . . . So then, my brethren, live."

3. *From:* Gerard Manley Hopkins, *Journals and Papers of Gerard Manley Hopkins,* edited by Humphrey House, completed by Graham Storey. New York: Oxford, 1959 (as reprinted in *A Hopkins Reader: Selections from the Writings of Gerard Manley Hopkins,* rev. and enl. edn., edited with an introduction by John Pick. New York: Doubleday, 1966), *the following (page nos. from Pick edn.): pp. 94–5,* [1870] "March 12—A fine sunset . . . square-cut in the original"; *pp. 106–7,* "[1872] Feb. 23—A lunar halo . . . ashes in our grove"; *pp. 161–66,* Oct. 12, 1881: To R. W. Dixon; *pp. 197–99,* Feb. 3, 1883: To Robert Bridges; *pp. 332–34,* June 4, 1886: To Coventry Patmore

4. *From* Gerard Manley Hopkins, *Further Papers of Hopkins, 2nd edn.,* edited by Claude Colleer Abbott. New York: Oxford, 1955 (as reprinted in *A Hopkins Reader: Selections from the Writings of Gerard Manley Hopkins,* rev. and enl. edn., edited with an introduction by John Pick. New York: Doubleday, 1966), *the following (page nos. from Pick edn.): pp. 135–38,* "Poetic Diction [An essay written for the Master of Balliol 1865 (?)]"; *pp. 138–40,* "All Words Mean Either Things or Relations of Things [Feb. 9, 1868]"

5. *From* Gerard Manley Hopkins, *Letters of Gerard Manley Hopkins to Robert Bridges,* edited by Claude Colleer Abbott. New York: Oxford, 1955 (as reprinted in *A Hopkins Reader: Selections from the Writings of Gerard Manley Hopkins,* rev. and enl. edn., edited with an introduction by John Pick. New York: Doubleday, 1966), *the following (page nos. from Pick edn.): pp. 185–89,* "Author's Preface [c. 1883]"

BRAD LEITHAUSER is the author of five novels, four books of poetry, a collection of essays, and *Darlington's Fall,* a novel in verse. He edited *The Norton Book of Ghost Stories* and *No Other Book,* the selected essays of Randall Jarrell. He was born in Detroit and attended Harvard College and Harvard Law School. He has been a Guggenheim Fellow and a MacArthur Fellow. He teaches at Mount Holyoke College and lives in Amherst, Massachusetts.

JOHN F. THORNTON is a literary agent, former publishing executive, and the coeditor, with Katharine Washburn, of *Dumbing Down* (1996) and *Tongues of Angels, Tongues of Men: A Book of Sermons* (1999). He lives in New York City.

SUSAN B. VARENNE is a New York City high school teacher with a strong avocational interest in and wide experience of spiritual literature. She holds an M.A. from the University of Chicago Divinity School and a Ph.D. from Columbia University.